NEITHER DO I

Victory Over Guilt, Shame & Condemnation

SHAMMAH GARA

NEITHER DO I: *Victory Over Guilt, Shame & Condemnation*

ISBN: 9798642318133

Unless otherwise indicated, scripture quotations are taken from the New King James Version (NKJV).

Published By: Handwriting of Heaven Publishing

Cover Design: Panashe Graphics

Photography: Tunde Osun Media

DEDICATION

Tiiana Anashe aka 'Tiia' aka my 'little cherry'… the sweetest girl there has ever been, with enough energy for two.

I love you with all of my heart & thank you for riding every day of those 9 months with me. You were the daily reminder of the strength I didn't know was available in God until I was left with no choice but to seek it. Most days it was just me, you & your powerful kicks from those adorable little feet I am obsessed by. A reminder that the life inside of me needed me to keep living.

I initially struggled to reconcile the testimony that this book is & the potential shock at some of the things that you will read. I wondered - Lord is this wise? But faithful as always, the Holy Spirit reminded me that obedience is always wise & that for the gaps and parts I cannot fill, my only obligation is to pray into them until the One who fills all things comes to do His work.

One day, your eyes will be able to read every word in this book. One day your heart will be able to understand the message in this book.

So I will pray for the next decade and beyond that the day you do, you meet the One I met when you were on the inside of me. The One who calls you Forgiven. Beautiful. The One who called you His.
His name is Jesus & He loves you more than I ever will.

Make it your aim to love Him more than anything on this Earth.

-Mummy-

ACKNOWLEDGMENTS

Abba: *Words rarely fail me but concerning this – they always will. So, I choose to let my heart, my will & my life reflect that here lies a grateful girl. A forgiven girl. Thank You for another chance. I Love You. Forever.*

Sis C: *The first person I told I was pregnant and the one to take me to my first hospital appointment. You told me: "Sis, everything will be alright. Do not kill this baby. It's not the end of the world." Thank you for being a big sister.*

Aunty Elizabeth Brown: *I am glad that I called you when I was almost going to cave to the pressure to abort. A woman of fire. Thank you for sounding the alarm. Tiiana is because you are and many will be because she is.*

Mum & Dad: *Thank you for not condemning me and reminding me that God still had a plan and a purpose for my life. Thank you for immediately proclaiming that abortion was not an option no matter the pressure I was under. Thank you for praying for me as I grew up – it works. It inspired me to war just as relentlessly for my children. Thank you for disappointing the crowd & popular opinion for the sake of God concerning me. It works. I have determined to do the same for my children as well. Above all thank you for dedicating me to God while I was still in the womb and making a covenant that has continued to speak over me even in places your hands and eyes could not reach as I grew up. What I once saw as an almost curse, being "marked for God" has often been the saving grace as to why I have come out of situations that have sent many to mental hospitals, their graves, and ultimately to hell.*

Thank you from the depths of my heart. May I grow to stand even half as tall as you did in the prayer room and on the battlefield.

Pastor Joseph & Mrs. Kudakwashe Dewah: *For me, your house was more than just a weekly accountability appointment. That cream sofa in the corner by the heater would often receive a very burdened and tormented young lady and her unborn child into its arms and each time she would rise from it a little more strengthened, a little more encouraged with a little more strength to go on. God bless you for pastoring me and praying for me throughout those 9 months and beyond. I remember your words Dad: "As for me, I am standing with you. Whoever asks me will be told I am standing with you!" May God reward you.*

Apostolic Faith Mission (AFM) Vessels of Honour Liverpool, UK: *For being a people of love who took out the 'law' in daughter in law. Thank you. I will forever cherish the beautiful baby shower you threw for me out of the love in your heart. You ministered to the shame ridden parts of me by celebrating the gift that my unborn baby was regardless of opinions. I also look forward to showing Tiia the pictures and the faces of the people who loved her before she ever was when she is old enough to understand. God bless you all!*

Pastor Sam Kuudzadombo aka 'Daddy Dombo' & Mrs. Rose Kuudzadombo aka 'Mum Dombo' : *The entire time I wrestled with what I had done and my sin, deep down my heart ached and longed for the One that I met for the first time in my life only when I walked through your front door: Abba. The revelation of God as my Father. Thank you for the haven your house was in the time I stayed there with you both. Because of you both, I learned to laugh again. I learned to trust. I learned to love both the Lord and His people. During those 9 months, I would remember and hunger for the encounters I had in my then bedroom. The*

God who visits His children and meets with them face to face. The One who comes and sits on their beds because He simply wants a chat, about anything & everything. The One who wakes them up at night just to whisper mysteries. One who hears every word and every cry. That God. I knew if I could somehow find Him again and lay ahold of Him then everything would be alright no matter what I had done. Thank you for giving me a reference point of God to long for during my pregnancy. For the times you taught me the Word of God from night till close to sunrise over many cups of tea and coffee, praying for me, fighting for me, and speaking life over my soul. Thank you. I made you so angry sometimes. You sowed. I did my own thing other times. You sowed. You never called me a bad name and you never raised your voice at me. You sowed. I will never forget that. For being one of the best earthly representations of my Heavenly Father, His love & His unchanging heart towards me – thank you. You introduced me to intimacy with Abba through the teachings you gave but more importantly through the way you lived your life. Thank you for leading me to discover my purpose in Him and also thank you from the very bottom of my heart for availing yourself to love a girl you did not have to and changing an entire generation by being used by God to first of all change me.

CONTENTS

INTRODUCTION..13

CHAPTER 1: WHAT'S DONE IN SECRET....................21

CHAPTER 2: REPENTANCE & RE-REPENTANCE........41

CHAPTER 3: TWO WRONGS DON'T MAKE A RIGHT...81

CHAPTER 4: SPREAD LIKE WILDFIRE.......................99

CHAPTER 5: ACCOUNTABILITY............................121

CHAPTER 6: STONE HER!..133

CHAPTER 7: TIIANA – A GIFT FROM GOD................153

CHAPTER 8: US VS. THE WORLD............................167

CHAPTER 9: TIME TO PUSH!.......................................183

CHAPTER 10: REFLECTIONS...................................191

CHAPTER 11: GIFTED..201

ABOUT AUTHOUR
GIRLS ON THE FRONT LINE

INTRODUCTION

I can only try to imagine the terrifying and lightning speed with which her emotions travelled from one end of the spectrum all the way down to the other. One minute she was gleefully exploring her illegal lovers' body with the same carefree delight a schoolgirl has as she walks out of class on the last day of Summer term. The next, she was being violently dragged through the dusty streets of the city to what was sure to be her certain death, her dirty little secret exposed for all to know.

Perhaps she had promised herself that today was going to be the last time as she snuck through the quiet streets earlier that day. Conscience in tow, "after this we are done", would have been the prelude to their sinful deed. Or it had been her very first time as she failed to resist the urge that continued to draw her to his charm day in and day out. Maybe there had been absolutely no intention of stopping whatsoever because after all, nobody but the two of them knew. Anyway, the details no longer mattered, it was too late. She had been caught. Red-handed.

Her journey came to an abrupt end & she found herself standing forcibly and struggling to catch her breath as the dust burned the insides of her throat. She was sure every bone in her body was close to broken – the pain was that intense. A crowd had formed a large circle around her & was jeering mercilessly as the seconds rolled by. Any time now, the show would begin. Face bowed low & covered by her tangled hair, she wondered where exactly they had brought her to.

"Whoremonger!" someone from her left shouted.

"Yes, she is a harlot!" another woman spat with rage.

"Adulterer. She must die!" She immediately recognised that voice. It was one of the Pharisees.

She fought back the tears from escaping her eyes. Partly from all the dust in the air that would not seem to settle but mostly from the fear and guilt that had slowly but surely began to invade her entire being. She suddenly became aware of all her emotions. She knew within herself that she knew better. Why had she done it? Had it really been worth it? They were going to kill her.

"Teacher... we caught her committing adultery not long ago today. Red handed as a matter of fact." Another teacher of the Law. This one sounded pleased. She winced in pain as the various cuts across her body, forcefully collected from the way they had hauled her through the dirt roads, began to sting. The crowd had become quiet now. Listening intently. This was going to be good!

"The law says we must stone her. Are you in agreement with the law?" She waited. The crowd waited. The leaders waited. Everybody waited. Silence.

Suddenly but also quite gently, she felt someone draw close to her. She dared to open one of her eyes and she watched as a man continued past her until He was crouched on the ground. He didn't look at her though. He didn't look at anyone. He simply wrote. The second her eye caught a glimpse of his face, the tears freely escaped from her eyes. She couldn't stop them now as the realisation that she was definitely going to die today sunk in. She knew Him. He was that infamous man who went around town & all the cities in the region doing mind-blowing things in the name of God.

The one that some even claimed was the Messiah. Others dared say that He was the Son of God. The audacity! She had been told that He was able to instantly cure people of their sicknesses and diseases & He had also challenged the Pharisees in ways everyone else only ever fantasised about. She knew exactly what He would say. He was going to agree with the law – adultery was a sin- and anyone with eyes could see and sense that there was definitely something peculiar about Him. An undeniable Holy aura. She on the other hand was unclean. She closed her eye again, accepting her fate. Oh, she was going to be brutally stoned. Today.

"Teacher. Do you agree with the law!?" The pressure and irritation in their voices cut through her troubled thoughts. Eventually, the Teacher stood up and finally, He spoke.

"Whoever has no sin between all of you gathered here today - let them throw the first stone at her."

The woman's eyes, still hidden, beneath her long dark hair, widened. Her head still bowed. She couldn't bring herself to lift it. She dared not believe. She was too ashamed. But what was happening? Was He defending her? Impossible! Had she misheard? Most certainly! Her eyes widened some more as she heard the sound of many feet shuffling. It almost sounded like people were leaving and as though the silent answer to His challenge from all present was "definitely not me." What was going on? She fought the glimmer of hope that had now began to flicker deep within her sinful soul. Who was He? Had she mistaken Him for someone else? The thoughts raced around her mind in a disorderly fashion. Finally, the shuffling came to a stop. Complete silence.

"Where are your condemners' woman? No one threw a stone at you?" His voice was strong but soft and with it came the courage she

needed to finally lift her head and look dead into the eyes of the man who held all her life in His bare hands. The One she was sure she recognised but clearly did not know. They were completely alone. The One who should have condemned her but instead stood looking at her with eyes of…what was it? Compassion? Love? Mercy? Grace? She didn't know but she knew she had never seen that look in any man's face before – especially towards her. He looked at her as though He knew her.

"There's nobody here but you & I." She croaked in disbelief. She suddenly felt a wave of nakedness sweep over her entire being but nothing like the usual because at the same time she had never felt more covered in her life. Something like an outrageous collision between beauty and ashes. Almost as though darkness was dissipating uncontrollably in the presence of light. And definitely the beginning of a divine exchange. Who was He? The circle had disappeared, and in its place stood the stones, a sinner & her Saviour. The perfect date with destiny.

"No one condemns me."

*"Then go and sin no more because **neither do I**."*

I find it interesting but not surprising that to this day we do not know the name of the woman who was caught in adultery in John 8:3-11. In fact, we know absolutely nothing about her apart from what she did. We simply know her by her sin and the weighty label as the woman who was caught in a sinful act but not so much the woman who was forgiven in-spite of the act or the woman she went on to be after her encounter with Jesus. Sadly, this gives us all a small insight into the nature of human beings sometimes, especially within the four walls of the church and just how easily who you are can become so insignificant when weighed against what you have done.

It seems to be much easier to label a woman as *"oh you mean the one who slept with all of those men?"* instead of her name. For some reason it is more satisfying to say, *"ah the womanising guy who cheats on his wife?"* instead of his name. It has become amusing and fulfilling for people who claim to be oh so dearly in love with Christ to be first in line to use terms such as *"Miss Whore"* or *"Mr Pinocchio"* as private jokes in their various circles instead of their names. And for a season it wasn't "Shammah" either, it was *"ah the pretend minister", "You mean Miss Hypocrite"* and many more unmentionable labels. But, there is hope and that is why I write this book.

I write to remind you that even though we will never know her name until eternity, we know His name. We know the name that is above every other name. We know the name that causes demons and all of Hell to tremble. We know the name that gives true freedom and liberty to all who will humbly ask for it. We know the name that brings total deliverance from guilt, shame and condemnation. We know the name that will go against the popular opinion to defend the lowly... wash you stain by stain & refine you blemish by blemish until every last one becomes as white as snow. It does not discriminate against height, age, race or background. The name that forgives ALL. The name that sees you for who you are and who it has called you to be from before the foundations of the Earth, not what you have done. The name that remains steadfast in the midnight hour, drying your unending tears when everyone else jumps ship, too ashamed to stand by you. The name that calls you into relationship, yes you & to your place of destiny. The name that when it is called upon, things that cannot be fathomed or imagined begin to take place.

The precious name of Jesus. Until His name, we had no name and without His name, we have no name.

It is my sincere prayer that through this book, every mislabelled person that has had their head bowed low in guilt, shame and condemnation will finally be able to raise it back up again towards Him. Towards Love. Towards Peace. Towards Strength. Towards Jesus, the only One in this entire universe with the certain right to throw the first, second and hundredth stone but instead continually chooses to whisper 3 of the most powerful words to have ever been said in history:

Neither Do I…

----- CHAPTER ONE -----

WHAT'S DONE IN SECRET

"OMG!" the young lady thought to herself as her eyes widened in terrified realisation and paralysed shock. The contents of the mug she was holding with her left hand almost drowning her mobile phone which was in her other hand.

"Umm, you okay Aunty?" It was her niece seated on the other side of the room, also with feet comfortably tucked into the sofa. She was looking at her with a mixture of curiosity & concern. The young lady frowned; she had heard her. How? She then realised she had actually voiced her secret thought aloud for the whole room to hear.

"I'm okay baby." LIE. She was not okay.

The intense & sudden eviction of virtue from her body that had led her to speak aloud had now passed but the message it had been sent to deliver, blue ticks and all was one she was not ready to accept at that current point of her life – not in a million years and yet deep down in her spirit she knew it was true. Very true. She sat for a moment longer quietly questioning her sanity. Yes, she was prophetic but surely she would have dreamt something in her dreams by now as opposed to relying on a fleeting sensation to inform her that her life was basically never going to be the same again? She began calculating the dates. Hopefully by the end of the week her cycle would come and…

"Girl…" She felt her heart begin to beat uncontrollably as truth gave her a side eye. There was no room for denial here. Still, she needed to be sure and there was only one way to settle this matter once & for all. In under 60 seconds she was dressed for the wind outside, sprinting her way to the nearest supermarket. The whole way there & back, a million thoughts raced through her mind all in complete contradiction to one another. She barely saw the traffic lights, dog owners or moving vehicles as her mind tried to envision what the result was going to be. Or rather what she desperately hoped the result would be.

She made it back home completely out of breath & went upstairs to confirm the unthinkable. She could not believe her eyes – so she ran to the supermarket again – made another purchase. Back up the stairs. Double confirmation. No! It was a lie. One last sprint to the supermarket… OMG. It was true!

The unmarried Christian Minister with an international girl's ministry, outspoken advocate for purity & holiness, born & raised in the church and mentor to so many young females was indeed PREGNANT.

That Summer day is a day I will never in all my life forget for as long as I live, for obvious reasons. How many girls can say that a sudden sensation in their body one day told them they were 100% pregnant before taking an actual test? Regardless, I was still shocked to see the positive pregnancy test before my eyes because of course the weight of a truth you suspect and one you know are two very different things. We were not married and so our goal had most certainly not been to be *"fruitful & multiply"* as instructed by God in Genesis 1:28. We were doing our own thing and as with all "own things" there were indeed consequences. My mind could clearly, as in CLEARLY remember the day, time & place we had done the deed – so what had I expected to happen? No, really… That the contraceptive pill I had made sure to take in secret would cover up my sin & I could carry on living my best life? Hmmm yes! Well, as long as whatever I was relying on was man made (the pill) it had the potential to fail and disappoint me especially if the aim was conceal immorality – and boy did it disappoint me indeed. 100%.

My heart has never & will probably never beat the way that it did in those seconds that I stood there with my mouth open in my bedroom staring at the pregnancy tests waiting for 'just kidding!' to appear on any of the screens at any moment to replace the extremely loud 'PREGNANT' that was looking back up at my face. That pill… what a let-down. Whatever happened to that 95% success rate?

Well, while I was wallowing in my self-inflicted disappointment, an even more important person had been disappointed by my actions: God. The truth is He has always had specific purposes for everything that He created. I knew this. So, I had done myself the greatest disservice by choosing to use one of His creations outside of His original intent for it. Sex. It was created by God for us to experience & explore in the safe confines of the covenant of marriage between one man and one woman. No other context has ever been acceptable to God. It didn't matter what culture declared or what society decreed – neither did it matter at all what my body was screaming out for. God's way for a thing should have been the only way for the thing.

On that particular day that was so deeply engraved in my mind, I didn't take the way of escape promised to me in 1 Corinthians 10:13 by either having a 3rd accountable person with me at all times, staying in a public and populated area or even sprinting out of the bedroom at the last possible millisecond in heed to that still small voice of warning that never stopped speaking. The voice that always speaks. It is no surprise then to anyone with sense that a few weeks later, a series of consequences and realities came knocking on the doorstep of my life starting with a set of very positive pregnancy tests.

My sin opened up a portal of many unpleasant things that I was in no way prepared for mentally, physically, emotionally, spiritually & every other "ally" you can think of. In fact, I don't think nobody can ever be prepared for the sudden twists & turns life can take when they choose to walk in direct disobedience to God. It's not something that can be pre-calculated neither should you ever think you are making an "informed decision" when you choose rebellion. My friend, you can never be prepared for the L's the devil will start dishing out to you with immediate effect. Everything I went through for at least the next 9 months had a direct link in one way or the other to the fact that I ignored God's original intent for sex.

The principle of consequences is one of the first things that is introduced to the majority of us by our parents or primary care givers from even before we can spell our own names. Insist on touching what you mustn't touch? A tap tap on the wrists. Think throwing a tantrum in the supermarket is cool? A butt whooping awaits. Caught in a lie? Privileges are withdrawn. And so forth. We quickly learn from a tender age that every bad action has an unpleasant result or sobering effect that eagerly accompanies it. These come in many shapes & sizes and they are certainly no respecter of persons. For some people, consequences seem to always be immediate and instant while for others it appears they "get away with it" – whatever *it* may be- for a longer period of time. However, I assure you that nothing and no one can stay hidden forever. We are firmly reminded of this in the Bible when it says: *"Do not be deceived, God is not mocked; for whatever a man sows, that will he also reap" (Galatians 6:7).* Whatever it is, eyewitnesses or not - it will catch up with you!

Often times as we find ourselves in the very thick of undesirable situations we usually forget this principle of reaping what we have sown as our outlook gets clouded with various emotions; fear, anger, pain, disappointment & shame to name but a few. Our world seems to spiral out of control & we desperately wonder: *"Why is God punishing me?"* Or *"Why has God allowed this to happen?"* forgetting to ask the most important question: *"What door has been opened to the devil through my own disobedience?"* We must always remember that the moment we move ourselves out of alignment of God's Word, Will & Way – we open the door up for the devil to fulfil his mandate: *"steal, kill & destroy" (John 10:10).* This has nothing to do with God. It is important for you to know that the enemy does not have rights to any area of your life without a door being opened up to him first -it's illegal. Your disobedience is the gold key that he needs to enter. Therefore, a daily lifestyle of obedience to God (something I was very much lacking in that season) protects you

& keeps him out. You are only safe when you live your life as God would have you live it. You are only safe when you follow the Word of God the way a young child does their mother.

This was probably one of the first few seasons in my life where the phrase *"why me?"* did not enter my mind and dare to come out of my usually outspoken mouth. I knew better than to try and pin this one on God. Oh, I knew so much better than that. The one million times my parents had taught me that sex before marriage was wrong told me I knew so much better than that. The sparkly ring on my right hand that symbolised the purity vow I had made freely in my own time before the Lord told me I knew so much better. The scores of young ladies who I had encouraged & strengthened in their own individual walks of purity with my self-published Dear Future Husband journal told me I knew. The many sermons I had preached & more told me I knew. As children of God - we always know.

Had I found the audacity go utter: *"Why did God allow me to get pregnant out of wedlock? Why didn't He just stop it?"* That would have been the height of irresponsible Christianity. As much as I sympathise with pain, the *"why me"* mentality in situations where we willingly open the door to the devil reeks of immaturity & pride. Excuse my bluntness. My relationship with God was in my hands. The notion that the definition of a "good God" is one that does what we want, how we want & when we want at the click of a finger without taking our actions into consideration is wrong! God sees everything and He is not a puppet. I couldn't secretly live my life as I pleased in direct contradiction to God's Word simply because there was no immediate human audience & expect God to be involved only when it came to publicly fishing me out of trouble. Sometimes the rescue from trouble is the exposure of your sin for the sake of your soul.

Even though we could never in a million years qualify or earn Him & His gifts. Our expectation from God must match our level of commitment to God as well as the depth of our covenant with God. In a similar way that we can only withdraw from the bank what we have put in. What I mean by that is that we have a responsibility to live in alignment to Him by the help of the Holy Spirit and in His Sovereignty, He handles the rest. "*Those who honour Me I will honour, and those who despise Me shall be lightly esteemed" (1 Samuel 2:30).* We have a part to play.

Revelations 12:10 makes it plain to us that the enemy works around the clock to bring forth accusations against us and there is nothing that makes his job easier than Christians who will not humble themselves and take responsibility. Blaming someone or something else for my pregnancy would have only delayed what I would have had to accept at the end of the day: I was pregnant and I needed to do something about it. Note that in Genesis 3:8-13 when God questioned Adam about what the forbidden fruit that he and his wife had eaten, he passed the blame onto Eve and she just as quickly passed it onto the snake. Also note that they did not escape facing due consequences just because they thought they had found the perfect scapegoat.

We partner with the devil against our own lives when we choose to beat about the bush instead of accepting our wrong and taking responsibility for it. He robs us of much needed time in the presence of the Lord seeking His wisdom and direction about our situation as we focus on everyone else but ourselves. I truly believe it is impossible to recover when you continue to live in denial. Satan can drive us to be -destructive of both self and others for as long as our fingers are pointed in the wrong direction. Stop. Take a look in the mirror and identify what you see.

I remember growing up & getting into a fight or argument of some sort with my siblings every once in a while. In a fit of tears and snot, one of us would then run to report the situation to either our Mum or Dad when we deemed that "enough was enough" only for them to do a thorough investigation & discover that the reporter was actually the instigator of the entire situation. Sound familiar? However, because s/he couldn't handle the outcome of the fight that they had started they had then decided to play victim. There would be no mention of their part or role in the whole story. Just a whole lot of she said, he said and she did, he did. You know it sounds familiar. The moral of the story being: the first one to cry is not always as innocent as they portray themselves to be.

This is not to discourage you from running to the Lord when you sin, quite the contrary actually. When we approach God in humility, only then can we reap the full benefits of The Cross. Humility is our way in. We must always do an honest self-check as often as possible -daily in fact - of all the different areas of our lives and honestly answer the following question: *"Am I committed to God and the standard laid out for me in His Word all the way in this area?"* In your finances, attitude, friendship choices, dressing, relationships, character, private devotion and more. If the answer is an honest no, just like mine definitely was in the season I got pregnant – you are opening yourself up to an almost certainly victorious attack from satan & his wicked kingdom which you will have to take responsibility for if you ever hope to recover.

Thankfully, God is so loving in that He will always come when we cry out for help via true repentance even in times of self-inflicted trouble. 2 Chronicles 7:14 says, *"...If My people who are called by My name will humble themselves, and pray and seek My face, and turn from their wicked ways, then I will hear from heaven, and will forgive their sin and heal their land."* However, more often than not we will have borne the consequences of our actions or still bear them in some shape or form after forgiveness.

As beautiful as the encounter was that the adulterous woman had with the Jesus in John 8, I can almost say for certain it would not have stopped the whispers from the people in the town over what she had done, the elbow nudges from passers-by each time she appeared in the market place or even tensions in her home and amongst her loved ones who would have felt much shame as a result of her actions. Those would have been her consequences to bear – yes, though her sins were forgiven.

God is not a genie or a fairy godmother - He is a loving Father & every good father wants their child to learn right from wrong – if not from directly heeding to their verbal/written instructions – then from first-hand experience through the repercussions that come with disobedience.

The absolute failure of that pill I took was my first lesson that there is never a "safe" alternative to disobeying God. It was also a sobering reminder that just because nobody knows about what I have done doesn't mean that it will never come out in one way or the other. Just the very thought of thinking I could get away with sin was foolishness but I didn't see it. My focus was to ensure our sin was only known to us so that life could move on quietly and peacefully. However, God created the creation that created that pill & there I was putting my faith in the lowest member of the hierarchy. Dumb. Instead of trusting in God who was more than able to *"keep you from stumbling, And to present you faultless Before the presence of His glory with exceeding joy" (Jude 1:24).*

I trusted the back-up plan for my disobedience. Well, good morning – class was now in session!

There is a saying that says: *"prevention is better than cure."* I wonder how many of you reading this are like how I was in that dark season of my life. How many of you would rather rely on a back-up plan to cover up your wrong (cure) instead of simply running in the opposite direction of committing that wrong in the very first place (prevention)? The woman in John 8 would have known that adultery ran the risk of getting her killed if she were to be caught because that was the Law of her culture but that did not stop her did it? I'm sure she and her lover had all of their measures in place: not making eye contact or appearing familiar with each other in public places and perhaps only meeting in the very dead of night before the sun rose or after the sun set. Instead of just good old straight forward obedience.

Why is an alternative to sold out submission to Christ always more appealing to us at times? Why does our confidence & pleasure in our sin increase when we are sure there is a solid backup plan in place to help fish us out of trouble should things go left? Are we actually trying to please God and live sold out lives for Him or we still have one foot in and the other out? Think just how differently we would live our lives if there was no such thing as a cover up or a back-up plan. I can assure you that my legs would have stayed shut, crossed and zipped if it was guaranteed that my belly would start growing with a baby the minute we finished having sex. If it was 100% guaranteed you paid for your sin within the hour you committed it would holiness & righteousness be more attractive to you then? Would you suddenly tap into the readily available strength of the Lord to stop doing those things that YOU do? I wonder when the goodness of God stopped being enough of a reason to live in

Holiness and Righteousness? How much more inspired would we be to do right if everything we did was immediately exposed for all to see?

This is why consequences are important. For the sake of our souls there are some lessons we have to learn even if it means learning them the hard way. There is no child that will ever mature, grow & develop the way they should without correction. It is also crippling to a child's development when a parent does every single thing for their child or comes to their rescue every second of every day. There has got to be a difference between genuinely helping someone and enabling them to the point of immaturity. We all know of certain people in our workplaces, schools and even families who have such an unbelievably entitled attitude, can't take no for an answer or live recklessly without much thought of the future. You know who I'm talking about. Them eyebrow raising individuals that leave you silently asking *"...and who exactly raised you!?"* All of these immature traits can be traced back to the improper foundation they were given by someone in their upbringing when it came to taking responsibility & facing consequences.

While God won't raise spoilt children, He will certainly raise disciplined and mature children. By this I mean children who reverence Him and understand that doing life God's way leads you down a certain path and ultimately to a certain destination as well as the fact that doing life the devils way also has a path it will lead you down. Children who understand that the difference between the two paths & end destinations is a six-letter word called CHOICE and that it is completely in their control. The same choice that Joshua proclaimed in Joshua 24:15, *"And if it seems evil to you to serve the LORD, choose for yourselves this day whom you will serve, whether the gods which your fathers served that were on the other side of the River, or the gods of the Amorites, in whose land you dwell. But as for me and my house, we will serve the LORD."*

Isn't it interesting how we love this word when we are justifying our actions and explorations of free will and independence – no matter how sinful & displeasing it may be to God - but we are suddenly silent about it when it starts birthing things, places, scenarios & people we never dreamed possible? *"At the end of the day, it's my choice..."* Ok. Fair enough but know that if your choice is not in line with the will of God, it will also soon become *your* pain.

God is a good Father. A very good Father. He can use whatever situations we find ourselves in for His ultimate glory if we allow Him to. Again, this is not a free pass to live how you want under the guise of "it will all work out one day anyway." Many have never recovered their hearts, minds and lives because of decisions they made that they did not realise would affect them in such a great way. Sin is never worth the risk.

In Hebrews 12:6, the Bible says, *"For whom the Lord loves He chastens [disciplines & corrects] and scourges every son He receives."* Because God is love (1 John 4:8) there is a big difference between the discipline of God & the condemnation of the enemy. When consequences start playing out – They are simply part and parcel of the principles of life. It is like throwing a ball in the air – it will come down. There is nothing spooky or deep to look for there because the principle of gravity stands and has jurisdiction. Period.

However, you have a choice as to who you align yourself with between God and the devil while those consequences play out and that is what determined how things will work out for you. I wonder what would have happened if the woman in John

8 had stood up and squared off with Jesus saying *"at the end of the day it's my body – I don't deserve death so yeah…"* instead of staying bowed at his feet. I believe her silence that day is something we can learn from. The fact that she offered up no defence for herself but quietly waited and then mercy was released is a message all by itself.

When I found myself in my situation or should I say when I walked right into my situation - being overwhelmed from every direction - God's intent and desire for me through it all was STILL for me to have an expected end. Jeremiah 29:11 still stood: *"For I know the thoughts that I think towards you says the Lord, thoughts of peace and not of evil, to give you a future and a hope."* Imagine that! He still had good thoughts for me & towards me however they were now going to have to be accomplished through a different route to His original intent for me because of my personal choices. You could call it a detour of sorts but a detour where one chooses to humbly surrender to the will and way God is a much better place to be in than going down the path of pride. In my situation it was the best place to be.

My out of wedlock pregnancy was not Heaven pointing down at me with a smug expression saying: *"Ha! See, we told you!"* as I know some were definitely itching to sing in my face at the time but had to settle for whispering behind my back. No, it was a consequence of my actions. Of our actions. The devil wanted me to believe that God had now washed His hands off me and given up on me completely with every fibre of my being – something I began to believe for a while during my pregnancy. An uncertainty over whose you are gives him access to feed you lies on who you are. And once the battle over your God given identity has been won by him – things become very dark from that moment on. He will do his best to lead you to obsess over

WHAT you have done (guilt), then feel worthless about WHO you are (shame) and lastly attack the assurance of WHOSE you are and His plans for you (condemnation). The devil is a liar. Heaven was saying, *"God can turn this around for good if you allow Him to Shammah."*

Even though it will never for a moment feel like it, God's discipline and correction as well as not intervening when some consequences begin to play out is always for the betterment of your soul. It is rooted in His unconditional love for you and its purpose is to grow you, mature you & ultimately bring you closer to Him than you were before things went wrong. It is for you to learn lessons – however difficult & long, come face to face with the true state of your heart & have God work His way in you until you are developed & truly transformed into His wonderful image. It is always for your good! Always.

The wake-up call that becoming pregnant was, shaped me for life in a way that sermons, church and even a spiritual title clearly had failed to do. God sees from a perspective that you and I will never see from because we are human hence Scripture says, *"For My thoughts are not your thoughts, Nor are your ways My ways," says the LORD. "For as the heavens are higher than the earth, So are My ways higher than your ways, And My thoughts than your thoughts" (Isaiah 55:8-9).* No matter what situation you find yourself in because of what you have done, what I have just described is how God wants things to go for you. Always. And they can. He is still in the business of giving beauty for ashes as promised in Isaiah 61:3.

On the other hand, the enemy desires to take advantage of whatever predicament it may be and use it to completely wipe you out, make you suffer endlessly & keep you from fulfilling your destiny through condemnation. Revelations 12:10 calls him the *"accuser of the brethren"* and he plays no games when it comes to attempting to capture a soul for his side. Satan does not like you – please understand that. He will swarm in with the guilt, the shame, the condemnation and everything else he possibly can to keep you stuck at the site of your sin instead of looking unto Jesus and the beautiful site where innocent blood was shed for that very thing you have done wrong: The Cross.

If he can convince you to blame God for consequences you invited into your life with open arms then he knows you will waste a great deal of time you could have spent humbly receiving mercy at the feet of the Lord. The more he can get you to focus on minors such as people gossiping and talking about you then the easier it is for your heart to harden against the Lord. Any route other than humility before the Lord allows a hardening of your heart to take place. Again, I am curious to know how things would have panned out if the woman caught in adultery had hardened her heart and chosen a different position in the face of the one person who could give her a fresh start. I wonder...

The posture of my heart during my pregnancy is what determined which of the two became my reality: God's discipline and it's beautiful ending if I faithfully stayed the course or the devil's condemnation & the deadly offers of escape that came with it. I had a choice to make and it had to be one or the other.

I could choose to be hard hearted, a blame gamer full of excuses & decide that what I was going through was "too much" according to MY standards. Which would have been an interesting conclusion to reach because when I fornicated I did not for a moment think I was doing "too much" against or towards God – the Omnipresent one who would have been a front row witness to our sin. I could have persisted in my sin and found myself farther away from God than I dreamed possible and certainly being defeated by the evil one. I would have also forfeited my destiny and proceeded to live a lifeless life. In essence, the posture I was going to choose was going to determine my future and the course of my life from that moment on.

Or I could be humble, giving myself in total surrender to the Lord no matter how bad and ugly the situation was & walk with Him step by step all the way through without taking any shortcuts. Only then would I come out of it refined, disciplined, more like Christ and with a powerful testimony to share of the mercies of God even though my entrance into the situation was through a wrongdoing on my part. The choice is yours.

In what I suppose was an effort to 'encourage me' I had some Christians – fellow ministers included - say things along the lines of: *"Shammah don't worry about it. There are other Christians who are fornicating repeatedly in secret, just that they haven't been caught. They are no better than you. In fact, they are worse! It's just that your sin is now public otherwise people are pretending to be self-righteous."* I later realised this was one of the greatest tests on what exactly were the contents of my heart. Who was my god? The praises of man or The Sovereign God? As some of the people tried to help me justify my sin, was I going to go with it or maintain the appropriate humble posture before God? I am sure the intent behind this was supposed to be pure however we must always be aware that many things will sound good to us but won't necessarily be godly.

I had my own personal relationship with God, though in that season it was ridiculously weak. How could I find comfort in the secret or public life of another human whose choices would not change the scripture in Romans 14:12 that says: *"So then each of us shall give an account of himself to God."* It didn't matter if these 'other fornicators' were Pastors, Bishops or respected leaders – I mean it could have been the Pope for all I knew but had the Lord returned for His people before I repented, I would not have been able to say: *"Yes I fornicated Lord but Sister A fornicated 15 more times than me, with 3 times the amount of men as well as on Sundays, your Holy day Lord! So surely I am spared!"* NO. Fornication was fornication! Fornication is fornication! Fornication will always be fornication. The Word of God had to be my point of reference as to what to do even after falling and not the life or words of another man. This is why the Word of God says, *"work out your own salvation with fear and trembling" (Philippians 2:12).* I had to focus on me and God and the ever-increasing nausea and growing bump were a daily reminder of this.

Sadly, many Christians fall into this trap and so they opt for burying their hearts and faces in the deep and quicksand of pride. It's like a toddler who covers their face with their hands thinking that because they can't see anything, they too are hidden. But God sees you. He sees us all. We must take responsibility for being in the wrong place at the wrong time. For our part in the conversation. For our part in the non-verbal communication. For our part in the hints we did not shut down. For our part in thought, in speech and in deed because when we don't we harden our hearts against the only One who can help us. Enough of colouring our unrepentant worlds with, *"I'm only human anyway nobody is perfect", "Cut me some slack, ministry/faith is hard", "I'm not the first or the last", Oh, it happens!"* and so forth. Sound familiar? Instead of remembering that *"God resists the proud but gives grace to the humble" (James 4:6).* -only the humble- and quickly taking ourselves to the presence of the Lord we resist God and still expect grace. Self-defence is the wrong response when you have sinned. So is silence. Running to God, His presence and His Word is your only defence.

I had to be sober minded and remember that *"So and so"* didn't die for me on the Cross or shed innocent blood for the very sin I was being presented with options on how to avoid confronting head on. When we fall short of God's standard we can only be truly restored *"If we confess our sins, He is faithful and just to forgive us our sins and to cleanse us from all unrighteousness" (1 John 1:9)* Not our Pastors sins. Not our neighbour's sins. Not the girl down the road's sins. If we confess OUR sins.

I need you to understand that another person's secret or public activities did not change that I knew for myself what the Word of God had to say about fornication and had directly disobeyed it. Another person's sins did not exempt me from facing due consequences. Another person's sins did not reduce the severity of my sin in the eyes of God. Another person's sins did not make the devil think twice before he joyfully somersaulted through the door I had opened to him and his wicked spirits and entities through my actions. I saw first-hand for myself what Ephesians 4:27 AMPC meant when it said, "*Leave no [such] room or foothold for the devil [give no opportunity to him].*" Now, imagine the devil's joy when all he knew he needed was a foothold to climb but I had gone off to give him an escalator ride up into my life. Most importantly, another person's sins did not change the fact that I, Shammah had personally & directly broken Abba's Heart.

I needed to quickly and genuinely accept responsibility for what I had done by repenting before the Lord and asking Him for the strength and wisdom to navigate the next 9 months and beyond no matter what came my way in a posture of righteousness. Yes, I could still be pleasing to the Lord and walk upright in the middle of my storm if I repented, growing belly and all. I could indeed reach a point of pregnant and righteous.

Victory over guilt, shame & condemnation starts with taking responsibility. You cannot be free from what you deny exists. You cannot be free from what you deny you caused. You cannot be free from what you won't accept you heard God warning you about, but you decided to go ahead anyway. You won't ever be free if you won't face the fact that if the devil is in – it's because you let him in. You cannot be free if you choose to bury your head in the sand. You will never be free if you choose to use every other possible label for what you have done *(weakness, I'm human, we all do it)* instead of calling it out directly for what it is: SIN. You won't be free walking around falsely comforted by convincing yourself that your secret sin is any less sinful than your neighbours' public sin. Your freedom starts with you!

So, there I was… saved, unmarried, pregnant & just like the woman caught in adultery: without an excuse…

In that order.

- It's better to run to God, His presence & word.
- Stop depending on the words of man.
- When we choose sin, we choose to not be in alignment with God.
- Be mindful of your relationships with God
- The enemy hates me and will do anything to mess me up!
- Examine your own salvation. Don't base it on what others are doing because one day you'll have to give an account to God!
- Take responsibility for what you've done
- E.g. Stop measuring your work ethic against that of others. by thinking you're ok to be lazy this time because you work harder than so and so
- Unless you face it you won't be free from it!

----- CHAPTER TWO -----

REPENTANCE & RE-REPENTANCE

The young lady fiddled with her fingers nervously as she waited in the queue to receive prayer & the guidance she so desperately needed. The conference had literally only just finished minutes ago and while others were happily taking selfies, catching up and sharing food - she had immediately made her way with full speed towards this power couple with her truck load of guilt in tow. Something about them had drawn her to them the previous day after a brief but powerful conversation in the car park & she knew that she had to speak to them before she lost her mind.

The deed of the day before continued to flash uncontrollably before her eyes. There was no getting rid of it. It was there in high definition and no detail was amiss. Oh my… She felt like a failure.

"How could you Shammah?" The voices silently cornered and spoke directly to her. Good question I suppose. She had broken her promise to God to live right, be right & do right – again - and now it was beginning to torment her. One more lady in front of her. Good.

"You promised didn't you? Again." The mockery was thick. She had nothing to say for herself so, she dug deeper into her fingers & began rocking from side to side. Anybody watching her intently would have been able to see that something was clearly troubling this young lady. She had made it through the remainder of the conference with a perfected exterior. The Pharisees would have been proud. Hands raised at the appropriate moments, dancing with her neighbours with a gladness that inspired several bystanders to watch her in admiration. Only she knew about the hidden guilt though. She looked up. It seemed the lady in front of her was almost done. Finally. Tears began filling her eyes & she looked around to see if anyone had noticed. She quickly caught herself. At this point who cared?

"How could you Sha-"

"Hello, how are you?" His deep but gentle voice broke through her troubled thoughts. She saw him notice the tears instantly & for once she was glad – it meant she didn't have to hide or pretend. She could simply be open. His wife joined him.

"Are you okay?" The wife hugged the young lady close as though she had known her, her whole life while he placed a firm hand on her left shoulder. And she sobbed. Without restraint. The salty flow on her face signifying the immense guilt that she carried. The couple waited. Patiently. As patient as the One who sent His Son to the Cross with no guarantee that you or I would ever accept Him and His shed blood. As patient as the father who waited for his reckless prodigal day in and day out with hope of his return deeply engraved in his heart. As patient as the One who didn't think twice about leaving the 99 to go after the 1. And as patient as the One who waited for every last accuser to depart from the woman until all that surrounded her were the stones. Stones and His presence. As patient as Jesus. As patient as Love. She broke the silence with a whisper.

"No. Yesterday I fornicated & I need to talk to someone"

The more I have grown in my walk with the Lord over the years, the more I have seen myself become transformed by the Holy Spirit into someone who is more often than not, quick to note and feel the pains of the Father when I do something that displeases Him and grieves His heart. It could be something as blatant as responding to someone with the finest clap-back of the century or as subtle (by human standards that is) as leaving my secret time of prayer with Him a little too early that day. Whatever the case, it is expected that the deeper you fall in love with someone – the more sensitised you become to their needs, desires & dislikes. It is a process but at some point you will find yourself naturally placing their preferences at the very forefront of your decisions, before your own and as a way of life until the line is so blurred that everything you do reminds every one of them. It's the proof that you value them. It's the proof that you highly esteem what the two of you have. It is also the tangible proof that who they are has begun to influence who you are.

Of course, there are also seasons of my life, like when I fell pregnant, where I have found myself shockingly distant from God's presence. The Proverbs 26:11 type of shockingly: *"As a dog returns to his own vomit, So a fool repeats his folly."* Ouch but true and I know that one or two of you reading this have been there too. In these moments God has not just been my last priority – He hasn't even been on the list of priorities. I mean, what else do you call living a life where you barely read your Bible or pray and sometimes not at all and you watch anything & everything as well as only involve Him in your decisions when is suits you. Let's call a spade a spade. He wasn't to be found on that list or even the reserve list.

My more important point, however, is that I think we can all agree that we are not drawn to people who are ignorant or careless when it comes to the issues that concern our hearts – I know I'm not. As a matter of fact, we naturally stay away from them and even go to the extent of cutting some of them out of our lives just to protect our hearts from the pain & drama that comes with associating with them.

We all sin more often than we care to admit & if the Bible says *"But your wickedness has separated you from your God, And your sins have hidden His face from you so that He does not hear" (Isaiah 59:2 AMP)* then what's the game plan to successfully maintaining a relationship with a Holy God when we are such a sinful people? What hope is there for us before this Great, All Powerful & Sovereign God? What hope was there for the woman caught in adultery? And what hope is there for the Christian girl who falls pregnant out of wedlock? Is it then not wishful thinking to believe that we can have a deep and intimate relationship with the Lord in spite of our flaws? Is there even a point in trying?

If you re-read the first sentence of this chapter you will note that I said that over time my sensitivity to the heart of Abba is what has strengthened and increased. I didn't say that over time I have stopped committing all sins known to man but that ultimately my heart response when I do, has changed. Now, before you conclude that I am giving you a green card to go off and sin – hear me out.

I sincerely believe that our power to completely stop is hidden in our ability to feel. The main issue in some of my seasons of immense distance between me & the Lord aside from what I had done and the way I was living was the fact that I didn't feel a single drop of anything about it. This desensitisation was as much of an issue as was what I had done and the sinful way in which I was living my life. The inability to feel.

Of all the characters in the Bible, one of my favourites would have to be King David. He was overlooked, despised & rejected by everyone around Him and yet ended up ruling over those very same people. It's the perfect rags to riches story and a wonderful example of what God can do with those who may publicly be unknown and ignored by man but are secretly known by Him in His presence. Of all the many exploits and achievements that David accomplished, the giants he slew, the cities he conquered, the fame and popularity he gained – The one that leaves me the most in awe as well as truly inspired is when we are told that God called Him a man after His own heart in Acts 13:22.

Take a moment to meditate on that statement. Imagine living your life in such a way that you capture the attention of the Creator of this entire Universe & He publicly announces you as someone after His own heart. This isn't a status that is reached with a one foot in, one foot out mentality when it comes to our walks with God. No this is another level. Think… how many humans can you personally speak about in such a way concerning your own heart? Dare I say they probably don't amount to the number of fingers you have on one hand! There are many nice, inspirational and compassionate people in all of our lives who we care for deeply but for one to earn the title as being one "after my own heart" that is another level of greatness & impact altogether. It takes a special kind of person to leave such an imprint on your heart to the point that it is written down on record & still spoken about thousands of years later long after they leave this Earth. Yet here we have a clearly imperfect man who made a mark on the one heart that matters above all other hearts. As faulty as David was.

If you look at the sins that he committed and this powerful statement that God used to describe him, you will find that the two are on complete opposite ends of the spectrum. That question arises again, how could there have been any kind of hope for such a sinful man before a Holy God? How could a murderer (2 Samuel 11:14-17), coveter (2 Samuel 11:2-5), adulterer (2 Samuel 11:3-5) and more be anything remotely pleasing to God? It simply doesn't make sense. I mean his track record made him a perfect candidate for those private joke labels I mentioned at the very start of this book.. Surely "Mr wife snatcher" was more befitting? It is rather unusual that such a life attached to a heinous track record of wrong could be praised and honoured by God in such a special way. Almost as shocking as those deadly stones that never ended up reaching the body of that adulterous woman that day. And definitely as shocking as the God who forgave me after I got pregnant out of wedlock. What was the missing link? What bridged the gap between David's sins and the pleasure that God still found in him?

Posture.

David was a man who had the ability to feel. The position, approach & attitude of his heart towards God after the wrong things that He did is what made God find such delight in Him. It showed someone who was humble & someone who took responsibility. It wasn't that his wrongs were any less wrong than my wrongs or your wrongs. No. Simply put, David was quick to run with his baggage to the feet of God in genuine repentance. He was quick to feel. He was a King but He didn't for a minute use that as an excuse to find an emergency exit from repenting as humbly as the rest of us are expected to when we sin against God.

There were no *"At the end of the day I am a King, what woman doesn't want to be with me? Of course, I get tempted!"* He had no pride to uphold in the presence of God. He had sinned. He acted accordingly.

He knew the only place He could be restored was in the Lord and that is where He made his abode. He would weep and groan before God as his heart ached not primarily because of what he had done but more-so WHO he had done it to. His greatest ache was the Lover He had disappointed – not the personal trouble He now found Himself in. In Psalm 51:4 he so beautifully said, *"...Against You, You only, have I sinned, And done this evil in Your sight..."* I believe that grasping this powerful truth with the fullness of our beings will change our relationships with God beautifully. Not a *"I've done this before God alone"* as an arrogant escape from human accountability, something I will touch on later. In fact, repentance done right will lead you to also make amends before man. I am referring to something that leads you to realise the gravity of your sin before a Great God who has done nothing but love you since you began breathing His air.

I said earlier that I believe that our power to stop is hidden and wrapped in our ability to feel. Please note that I am talking beyond a tangible sensation of guilt and a self-centred cry of "Oh no! what have I done?" This is not about your emotions. This is not about people. This is not about YOU. God is not impressed by theatrics.. He also knows when your repentance is actually just masked regret. I am not referring to goose bumps or a lump in your throat either. Nor am I referring to piano music assisted tears or fleeting butterfly like sensations in your tummy in the middle of a powerful conference. When I say our ability to feel I speak of feeling Him. I speak of feeling His Heart. I speak of the fear of the Lord. I speak of feeling Jesus.

The Bible says: *"The LORD is near to the heartbroken And He saves those who are crushed in spirit (contrite in heart, truly sorry for their sin)" (Psalm 34:18 AMP).* Until you're crushed you cannot be saved. Until you're crushed, you cannot be free. I've never known anything to be crushed without there being a loud sound of some sort being released from it & a clear undignified destroying of the shape & form it once was. It's not a crushing if it still looks the same. It's not a crushing if it still walks the same. It's not a crushing if it still sounds the same. It's not a crushing if it still maintains its dignity. Are you following me?

Perhaps the reason why your sins continue to haunt you in one way or the other is because you don't sit in the presence of the Lord long enough for him to utterly destroy everything in you that keeps longing for your old way of life. Perhaps your posture is all wrong. I know mine certainly was The less time I spent kneeling before the Lord, the more my strength to stand against temptation grew. Perhaps you are yet to be truly crushed concerning whatever it is that you have done. You safely tuck away the vomit as a just in case so that you can go back to eat it up as though it were a 5 start 3 course meal in case you need it the moment you are lonely, insecure & wanting something to make you feel valued & important. For the moments when you feel you need an escape from the realities of life. For the moments when anything to do with God seems like a chore. For the moments when everything but God has an open-door policy to fill the voids in your heart.

You don't sit long enough at the faithful feet of Jesus on a daily basis to be crushed (confronted, convicted & changed) until the only song & sound your life is able and willing to make is one laced with evidence of a newfound and genuine sensitivity towards the Lord's heart above all else. A heart that feels, in order to stop. Something is always more important to you. My then boyfriend was. More urgent. My boyfriend's phone calls were. More deserving of your feel. My boyfriend's body over the Lord's heart eventually was. And so while there has always been a point in trying & while there is hope for us all no matter what sin we commit because of the Cross of Calvary, just know that it will require all of the humility in this world and an understanding that without a crushing & a violent rearranging of your priorities there can be no saving from the sin that plagues your life.

In the previous chapter I spoke about consequences. Understand that in the series of all the consequences I had to deal with in the months following my act of fornication, the greatest was not the fact that I fell pregnant out of wedlock. It was definitely a consequence just not the most important.

I know that in the church, definitely culturally (I was born in Zimbabwe, Africa) & in many other parts of society we have been led to believe that the worst thing that can happen to a female that fornicates is a pregnancy. Wrong. It's also the picture that a few people tried to paint so vividly for me repeatedly throughout my 9 months. Though ashamed, I silently knew better. I knew that this mentality was and is rooted in pride, the fear of man and ultimately a lack of reverence for God. A lack of feel. Such a mind looks at the effect that their sin personally has on them, their life, status, ego & reputation. The posture is all wrong.

Now I am not turning a blind eye to some of the realities that inconveniently unfold as a result of an unplanned pregnancy. For some, studies have to be postponed temporarily or even permanently. Dreams, plans and visions fade off into the far distance sometimes never to be recovered. For me, I had to relocate to a city away from all of my loved ones. I wasn't able to work. My plans to pick up my studies again because I was now sure of what I wanted to study, had to be aborted and so many other changes that turned my world upside down. All of this is very real but when it becomes placed on a pedestal before God we have a problem. Our posture becomes a problem.

This posture resists God. This posture is also responsible for the teaching in homes, churches, schools and more worldwide that teaches our sisters, daughters and nieces and says they must abstain from fornication in order to avoid getting pregnant out of wedlock as opposed to the fact that they must pursue purity in order to please the heart of God. The two are not the same thing. I remember being angrily told to my face at some point during my pregnancy: *"Do you know what you have done to ME with this pregnancy? What the two of you have done to ME!"* Nothing about God. Nothing about my relationship with Him. Nothing about my soul. Posture.

As Christians we are not called to live our lives in some sort of religious trepidation as though we are walking through a minefield because at any moment there can be an explosion that will cause disappointment to us and the humans in our lives if we dare make a wrong step. NO! This is also not a free pass for us to take sin lightly either. My point is that sensitivity to the heart of the Father is the goal not a life ruled by fear & suspicion because wrapped in that sensitivity is the strength you and I need to overcome sin. We are invited to walk lovingly & submissively hand in hand with Jesus following His lead in full confidence that He will never lead us astray and that for as long as we are by His side, submitted to Him, His Word & His Ways and listening to His heartbeat, we can have certain victory over sin. *"Now to Him who is able to keep you from stumbling, And to present you faultless Before the presence of His glory with exceeding joy" (Jude 1:24).* The question is do you WANT to be kept? If so, it cannot be according to your specifications of being kept. It's according to the Lords.

A true lover of God who is sensitised to His needs and desires looks at the effect sin has on their relationship with God and the heart of God. It is not about their title, their position, reputation or their influence first - IT'S ABOUT JESUS! It's not about what people will say, do or think first – IT'S ABOUT JESUS!

My relationship with God drastically deteriorated in the months that followed and had been for a good while prior. I am talking riches to rags, if that at all because at least with rags there is something for one to still work with. I lost it all. I was already not where I was supposed to be spiritually because I got pregnant in the first place & things just took a nosedive from then on. The hours of intimate prayer dwindled down to silence. I was so ashamed I didn't even know where to begin. It was the kind of shame that you feel physically and we were as inseparable as a mother and her babe. It was like there was a clamp over my mouth & while I knew I should pray I could not do it. I wouldn't do it. Why on Earth would He listen to what I had to say? I hadn't listened to Him! This was the biggest mess up of my life and by now I was sure I had used up all of my chances with a God who had given me a fair share of them over the years.

The hours of Bible Study were reduced to liking the occasional Christian quote on Instagram every few days. The pages of my Bible almost felt extra heavy whenever I tried to open them as thoughts of worthlessness cheered me on. Tears would fall from my eyes onto the pages until I couldn't see anything and so, I allowed it to gather dust in my room. Then I REALLY couldn't see. *"Your word is a lamp to my feet And a light to my path" (Psalms 119:105 AMP).* I allowed Life to gather dust as I died spiritually day after day. "*The words that I speak to you are spirit, and they are life" (John 6:63).* I neglected the very thing I needed to revive my sinful soul and the fragmented pieces of my heart. A severely sick patient who so desperately needed to get well again but still somehow thought she knew better than the Doctor. A girl after her OWN heart...

The regular walks with the Lord talking about anything & everything and making plans months and years in advance were replaced with anxiety filled walks to escape bullying, verbal abuse & physical abuse and filled with a focus on self and just how terrible my life had become. I wasn't automatically humble just because I was ashamed. Pride still had a seat in my heart. The sceneries of nature that once inspired uncontainable melodies and songs from the depths of my spirit dried up. The birds were better off than me. Even the trees looked happier as I walked around the block with my growing bump day after day. The only song to be heard being the enemy's victory chant over my soul.

The only way for me to express it to you is that there is nothing like missing the one that you love. Many years prior I had refused to settle for an ordinary relationship with God. Flashbacks of feeling the Lord wrap His presence around me in moments of worship in my bedroom presented themselves. Thoughts of the times I would lock myself away for no less than 3 hours at a time clearly stating I was not to be disturbed because God was calling me came to the forefront of my burdened mind. The times I would ask God questions silently about the most random of things and later that day He would send an answer via a friend, the news, my Dad or an article I would stumble across circled my mind. The God who had restored so much of what I had l lost in my childhood came up. The day a wind blew in my bedroom during prayer though all the windows were closed as a sign from the Lord came up in my mind. The God who had held me in His arms in seasons of brokenness , I often thought of.

The day I smelt a sweet fragrance gently invade my room during worship though I was certainly alone came up. Memories of the Holy Spirit waking me up in the middle of the night to write a message to His people on my Instagram page replayed themselves. This God has been so faithful to me, true to His covenant. I had not. I sank deeper into shame missing the point that these memories were Abba's way of reaching for me while the enemy used them to torment me. There is nothing like breaking the heart of the One you love. There is nothing like missing the One you love.

I would sit in church hearing nothing and only feeling absolutely nothing but the nausea swishing around in my belly waiting for the most inconvenient moment to erupt. It was like a numbness settled over me. Each time God called me and tugged at my ever-hardening heart to retreat into His presence whether it was in the middle of the day or the middle of the night – I delayed in responding by days because shame and fear would grip my heart so violently until I stopped responding altogether. This is when we see that knowledge isn't necessarily power. The knowledge that you act on is power. Obedience is true power.

Unsurprisingly this neglect of my walk with God opened me up to various spiritual attacks: endless nightmares at night as so many weird, dark & ghastly looking beings would chase me, beat me and torment me in my sleep. They would throw things at my belly in my sleep, try to poison me, try to shoot my belly and on and on. There is nothing that they didn't try. And for months I took every defeating blow in silence aware that I did deserve it but also unaware that the beginning of freedom was a simple decision away. I would occasionally fantasise about a happily ever after on the days I could find a little positivity to dwell on but my future was dependant on what I did with my mouth. For as long as I was quiet – I was bound. That, my friends was the greatest consequence of that season. The gap between Jesus and I - not the growing bump.

I was well aware of the power and danger of silence especially when it comes to things that happen in secret which is why I initially approached this couple who were Pastors on that particular Sunday afternoon. The day after we did the deed. The conversation we had in the car park had entailed of the husband saying something along the lines of *"Your destiny is so bright and great. When I look at you I see a part of your calling and the mandate to raise women of Purpose. Women of a high calibre"* Can you believe that? On the way to a room we were going to "chill" in God still found a way to speak to me through a couple I had never met prior to that day. He tried to warn me. He really did. Using love as His language. I paid no attention. I didn't even notice that He was speaking to me that way – only much later did I realise as me and my growing bump became familiar with each other.

I knew that I didn't want to carry guilt home with me. So, I confessed honestly and openly. After all, the Bible does encourage us to *"confess your trespasses to one another" (James 5:16).* At no other time in my life had I ever felt so strongly to go and speak to a stranger about a sin I had committed. In hindsight, I sincerely believe that it was the Lord's kindness that prompted me to do so because though nobody knew -myself included- at the time, that the deed from the day before was going to result in pregnancy, their words that day were a much welcome replay in my mind during my pregnancy. They listened and led me through a prayer of repentance and encouraged me to press on in my walk with God and maintain the physical boundaries in my relationship.

I left the conference feeling relieved and somewhat better about myself. What I will never forget was their approach as I stood there relaying what was the cause of my distress. They didn't judge me. Neither did they make me feel anymore guilty than I already did. They didn't even side eye each-other in that coded way that only a husband and wife can. They simply listened. They directed me to the Word of God with such love and grace & reminded me that God was still in love with me – though displeased with what I had done, I was deeply loved. I want to dwell here for a moment.

Do you know that you loved by God? He gave everything so that you and Him could be in relationship forever. He initiated. He led. He showed the way. He is in love with you and I know that when we are in a world that can be so cruel and out to use you before dumping you to the side, this can be an almost impossible truth to believe. But it is true. God loves you. He loved you in your sin and He loves you in your sin which is why He so desperately wants you out of it. Love is what binds everything that I talk about in this book together. *"We love Him because He first loved us" (1 John 4:19).* God waits for your just like He was waiting for me.. The 24 hours I had spent from the day before wallowing in my own guilt had been 24 hours too long. I should have gone to God immediately & began my repentance there and then.

So, what is repentance?

It simply means to turn away from your sins and turn to God. We turn away from our sins by confessing them to God in prayer and asking for forgiveness. God does not need 5 working days to decide if He is going to forgive you. Humbly ask and you will receive. 1 John 1:9 says, *"If you confess your sins, He is faithful and just to forgive us our sins and to cleanse us from all unrighteousness."* That is a sure thing as well as a free gift we are given by our Heavenly Father. You cannot earn or work for God's forgiveness – you can only be given forgiveness freely from the heart of the Father when you ask by faith. No matter what you have done – if you go to God and ask for forgiveness, He will forgive you. Sex outside of marriage? Forgive-able. An abortion? Forgive-able. Pornography? Forgive-able. Drugs and alcohol? Forgive-able. Rebellion? Forgive-able. Masturbation? Forgive-able. Judging other people's public sins? Forgive-able. The very second you repent – You are forgiven.

Some Christians think that as long as enough time passes between the wrong they did then it is forgiven and forgotten about. Wrong. Others think if they fill their schedule with church activity & things that they deem to be "good deeds" then all is forgiven and forgotten. Wrong. Some also think that if human beings, especially Christian human beings or their loved ones show them support even in the face of their sin then God has also automatically forgiven them. Also wrong. If you do not have a specific moment, when you open your mouth and confess the sin you have committed to God audibly e.g. fornication, lying, gossiping, stealing etc… from a place of genuine repentance then it has not been forgiven. It's that simple. Hence the term "unconfessed sin" exists. We mustn't mistake the fact that our schedules, careers and lives as we know them have continued to advance and maybe even excel as a sign that we are in right standing with God. It does not matter how much time or church events have passed since your sin – it is not forgiven! Unconfessed sin opens doors to the enemy.

In the book of Joshua 7 we read the sobering story of man called Achan. I won't narrate it in full because I want to encourage you to open the Bible and read the Word of God for yourself. The sin he committed not only affected him or his family but the entire nation of Israel even though it was only known to him. He thought he had gotten away with it because it was hidden from human sight. Achan forgot that God sees everything and God knew exactly what He had done and that was the most important thing to be feared. While the multitudes were none the wiser, the greater audience of One was in the know. Unfortunately, for as long as His sin remained hidden and unconfessed, the entire nation suffered for his wrongdoing and they experienced defeat after defeat at the hand of an enemy they should have easily been able to defeat. The first time Israel encountered a loss in the face of this enemy should have prompted Achan to come forward and reveal what he had done but he didn't therefore one man's refusal to be crushed caused and entire nation to continue to be conquered. Consequences were still faced even though he was the only human in the know about what he had done secretly. It wasn't until His sin became exposed and he finally confessed that the nation was finally able to possess God's promises.

Some of the things that are continuously going wrong in our lives and the people connected to us and the circles that we seem to forever be going around in and the lack of breakthrough in certain areas of our lives, families, finances, health and so forth are for the same reason: we have unconfessed sin that we think doesn't matter either because nobody but us knows about it or a lot of time has passed since it happened. We even have a bag of excuses to justify why we did what we did. Time has moved on. Life has moved on so everybody has moved on. Incorrect. God has not moved on which will explain why your life has not moved on.

I remember one of the things I immediately did as my relationship with God began to decline and die was to release all of my ministry team members, volunteers and workers and putting a pause on my girl's ministry as a whole. I knew that I couldn't carry on and while it was a wise gesture on the outside I still hadn't taken myself in humility to sit at the presence of God. It was a religious act because I still accepted ministration invitations that had me appearing on flyers, I just didn't want to lead a team and be accountable in that way. It was almost as if the ministry work was the big elephant in the room that reminded me of my guilt more than anything so it was better to put a pause on things for a while. I was running away from the crushing. The Bible even goes to the extent of saying the following:

"He who covers his sins will not prosper, but whoever confesses and forsakes them will have mercy" (Proverbs 28:13).

"When I kept silent about my sin, my body wasted away through my groaning all day long" (Psalm 32:3 AMP).

"If I regard sin and baseness in my heart [if I know it is there and do nothing about it] the Lord will not hear me" (Psalm 66:18 AMP).

We can see for ourselves the importance of confessing our sins before God. It is not enough to know about it if you don't do something about it. *"And there is no creature hidden from His sight, but all things are naked and open to the eyes of Him to whom we must give account" (Hebrews 4:13).* A sin committed in a pitch-dark steamy room, although hidden from man and those who know you best is seen in high definition by the eyes of the Father. He is the One that truly matters. You cannot run.

When I found out I was pregnant the guilt that I thought I had left at that conference firstly in that bedroom and secondly in the presence of those two Pastors weeks prior, returned all over again. Hold on… what? Yes. I am talking fresh guilt. On top of that the more the news of my out of wedlock pregnancy began to slowly trickle out to the public – my shame intensified. I even remember a woman who took it upon herself to send me the pregnant woman emoji in my DM. Not a single word just emoji after repeated emoji after emoji as she taunted me and the years of her secret dislike for me finally had a stable stage to parade across. I literally wanted to bury myself alive at that point.

So, had I not repented? What was it about the knowledge of a physical consequence I could now touch, see and feel as time passed by that seemed to put me back at square one in terms of my emotions and mind? Was my sin now more severe because people had found out about it & I was about to embark on a 9 month journey that would be a daily reminder to anyone with a working pair of eyes that I had indeed sinned once upon a time? I had repented, or so I thought and even walked away from that weekend feeling somewhat lighter so how could I now be feeling condemned for something that I had already been forgiven for? For something that was surely deeply swimming away in the *"sea of forgetfulness" (Mark 7:19).*

Let's go back to the definition of repentance a few paragraphs back. It means to *turn away from your sins* AND *turn to God*. The second part of that definition: *turn to God* is what I didn't do much about and what many Christians fail to apply properly in their lives. Unless the confession of our mouth is coupled with total surrender from the heart – we have wasted our breath. Unless our admission is coupled with submission – again we have wasted our breath. Remember it is all about posture. Repentance goes beyond "I'm sorry – forgive me." If anything, that's the start of it all. In the story of Achan, it was not enough for him to confess when he eventually did. There was a step after confession.

One of the most profound and unforgettable things that someone ever said to me via a Facebook messenger conversation during my pregnancy as I broke down one day after another day full of blows of defeat from guilt, shame & condemnation, was the following statement: *"Shammah, It's not about showing God you've repented by not fornicating. It's about getting more intimate with HIM than you used to be before fornicating. That is what real fruit of repentance is."*

WOW! I immediately realised that my focus had been completely wrong. I was obsessing over what I had done and all of the many ways I could ensure to the best of my ability I did not do it again. Meanwhile God was simply waiting for His lover to come back to Him. It was all about being restored back to HIM. That is what it has always been about. It was not about getting myself back to that place of boasting with "I have not had sex for 5 years or 3 years or 6 months yay look at me" as some do meanwhile their private relationships with God are on zero. It was about getting back to the Lord.

Consequently, the reason we have a generation of Christians who can't STAY away from sin after seemingly turning away from it is because – they don't TURN TO God. If you turned to Him He would give you His heart & you'd begin to have the same disgust & hate for sin as He does. That's that feeling I was talking about. The feeling that enables you to stop. The feeling that means you immediately ache at whatever aches the heart of God. The feeling that means you are now unwilling to allow anything to get in-between you & God: every boy, every friend, every porn video, every conversation. Anything and everything. The feeling that goes beyond changed behaviour & actually leads to genuine fruits of repentance being produced in your life. The feeling that leads to a total upside down inside out transformation of your heart.

It's easy to reach a point of confessing your sins if the atmosphere is emotional enough and the right chords are played to stir you to the point of tears and a form of remorse. This is why we then find ourselves back at square one either doing that same thing again and still walking around in condemnation is because we are simply not turning to God. We have all given an apology to someone that we really did not mean at one point in our lives usually to shut them up and keep them from nagging. Similarly, we are merely confessing enough to be forgiven by Him but not surrendering enough to Him to be transformed by Him.

A lot of us will put in sin management measures fuelled by our own self-determination instead of complete submission to the Holy Spirit then wonder why we continue to be trampled by that which we as children of God are supposed to trample over. If it is the sin of pornography we will throw away all of the filthy magazines and books we own - forgetting that a shredded magazine in a bin does not evict the spirit of lust from our lives or heal the childhood trauma of rape or molestation that led to this sin. The presence of God does.

If it is gossiping, we will try to minimise the amount of time we spend talking to certain people or change our friendship circles – not realising that fresh faces or a new number will not uproot the spirit of jealousy & comparison from deep within our souls. The Holy Spirit does. Then a few days, weeks or months pass and we find ourselves doing the very thing that we put our best man-made efforts into never doing again. Why? Because we put our focus on the first part of the definition of repentance: *"turning away from sin"* and forget that the only thing that can keep a Christian turned away from sin consistently is a life that is deeply and consistently *"turned towards God."* It's not enough to turn AWAY from without turning TO. Unless you are planted in Him, you can't produce anything of Him. Never has fruit appeared from thin air. Only that which is first planted is a candidate to produce and each will always produce after its own kind. The Bible says in John 15:4, *"Abide in Me, and I in you. As the branch cannot bear fruit of itself, unless it abides in the vine, neither can you, unless you abide in Me."*

There is more power in a genuine desire rooted in love to please God than a self-based determination to stay away from sin. To think that you have the power to live in holiness by your own strength is an unprecedented form of pride and foolishness and boy was I was the Head Prefect in that school. The basis of everything we do for God must be our love for Him – nothing else and you can't fall in love with someone you don't intentionally spend time with. The only antidote for sin is Jesus Christ and when we fail to turn to Him – the devil will happily & most eagerly give us something else to turn to. Anything but Jesus will do for him! In John 14:15 Christ said: *"If you love Me, keep My commandments."* He didn't say if you are determined or afraid of what people will say about you, He said if you LOVE Him.

If I am to be honest, my relationship with God did not particularly change much after the conference. If anything, it actually worsened. I remember determining to read a devotion recommended to me by that power couple and it only lasted a few days. My mind was simply elsewhere… Remember I said that I left the conference feeling better about *myself.* I didn't leave with a burning desire or decision to study my Word more and go deeper in God. I didn't cultivate a deeper pursuit of Jesus. I simply continued exactly how I was prior to the conference. There wasn't any "turning to" the Lord, on a deeper level in any way. Yes, I still prayed and read my Bible but no more intensely than before. Instead, I pinned my hopes more on the fact that me and him lived many miles apart, an overnight weekend event was probably never going to happen again until 'this time next year' at the next conference and so by then I could have found some friends to go with me or we would have hopefully become stronger at resisting temptation. It's funny now looking back but the foolishness…

While I prided myself in physical boundaries, distance & an emergency 3rd accountable person to be present for the 'next time' as my so called fruits of repentance – God was patiently waiting to find me at His feet and in His presence more frequently because we were in relationship but also because He knew what was waiting for me around the corner and He wanted to prepare and strengthen me. He had more than a few hard truths about me to reveal to me and work out in me that went far beyond ending up in a bed with a man that was not my husband. He wanted to heal me, strengthen me & show me the true state of my heart – yes even as a minister. In fact, especially as a woman of God. But I was busy doing other things.

I was busy watching TV & YouTube videos, I was busy going shopping & eating out. In fact, I remember being particularly obsessed with the growth of my natural hair, edges and all in that season which had really taken to the new products and regime I had found. I literally spent hours (when all added up) in front of the mirror looking at myself. I was busy relating with Him on the 'usual level' – sometimes not at all depending on the day and my schedule - I was busy living my best life, hanging out with friends, posting Christian quotes, attending church and interestingly, I was also busy doing the work of the ministry as a minister. The gift flowed as I died. Everything but deliberate, set aside time with Him broken at His feet confronting uncomfortable truths about the distance between where I once was in relation to Him as a Christian and where I currently found myself. Everything but being crushed. It was still all about me and not the fact that I broke the heart of Abba, the One I said I loved by doing what I did.

This is when I must highlight the dangers of being able to operate in your gifts from God even though you are no longer pleasing in His sight. *"For the gifts and the calling of God are irrevocable" (Romans 11:29).* This is when the dangers of having a social media following that you publicly get applause from because the majority can't for a moment begin to fathom that the woman of God is not in right standing with God. *"But the LORD said to Samuel, "Do not look at his appearance or at his physical stature, because I have refused him. For the LORD does not see as man sees; for man looks at the outward appearance, but the LORD looks at the heart" (1 Samuel 16:7).* This is when the dangers of flowing in power when you have lost the presence must be talked about. This is when you pause your reading and do a heart check. Where do you stand!? Be honest.

Do not get me wrong – the Pastors I confided in are not to blame for this lest we miss my entire point completely. They did their part as led by the Holy Spirit. The same part we all have to play if someone ever confides in us about something that they have done which is to extend love & show them Jesus. He is their Saviour. He is their judge. Not you. However, it was all entirely up-to me to think how much I truly valued my walk with God from that moment on. *"Therefore, my beloved, as you have always obeyed, not as in my presence only, but now much more in my absence, work out your own salvation with fear and trembling" (Philippians 2:12).*

Nobody could give me a passion for God – I had to allow the Holy Spirit to cultivate it in me through daily submission to Him. Nobody could open my Bible for me – I had to study it for myself. Even if somebody prayed for me, as they did on that precious day, that could never replace the act of opening my own mouth and crying out to God by myself. Think about it, if the state or level of my relationship with God prior to fornicating was at the right level in the first place then I wouldn't have committed the sin I did. Hello! That in itself was a sign that I needed to level up and go deeper. But I didn't. I was content with the verbal part of repentance and not the heart part. My whole life at that point had gotten down to everything verbal and nothing more.

This is why guilt, shame and condemnation had a field day with me when I came face to face with a tangible consequence of my sin. This is why the moment people began to find out – though many months later – it felt like I had just committed fornication that very morning & every single morning after that. I was easily shaken because although I was deeply loved by God I was no longer rooted in God. It doesn't matter how tall a tree is – if it has weak roots then even a babe can knock it over, how much more gale force winds like the ones I was facing. This is why I walked in defeat for many months. I did not complete my repentance.

Turning away from my sin meant I was forgiven of fornication – 100% - but my failure to fully turn to God meant that I missed the bigger picture. I missed God's perspective. While all I saw was the sin of fornication, He saw the sin of prayerlessness. The sin of idolatry. The sin of pride. The sin of ignoring His tugs on my heart. And many other sins that all led up-to what I and many others only considered to be the "big sin." It is all sin! It also meant I had no strength or stamina to stand when the consequences attached to my sin came my way. It meant my mind had not been renewed and it could easily be tossed to and fro by anything the devil fed and whispered to me. It meant my heart had not been dealt with. It meant that for a season my consequences conquered me instead of creating a Christlike nature in me through surrender to the Holy Spirit.

Forgiveness from sin doesn't automatically mean strength. It simply means we are pardoned from spending eternity in Hell separated from God. It means there is no longer a record of our wrongdoings and it means you instantly have peace with God. However, in order to receive strength as well as the restoration of our hearts, minds and the transformation of our character that is something that you and I need to purposefully position ourselves for to receive by turning towards Him and seeking Him continually in our secret place.

In Isaiah 40:31 renewed strength is only promised to those who will wait upon the Lord. It does not say those who are forgiven – but those who wait. We have too many forgiven but fast people. People who won't wait. To wait: continually going to His presence to spend time with Him as His pace and hear His heart, His thoughts and His specific instructions for you. However, the reason that many of us are unwilling to do this is because it involves sacrifice and a rearranging of our priorities, schedules and a forsaking of our idols.

"You shall have no other gods before Me" (Exodus 20:3). For the majority of us this means the boyfriend has to go.The friends. The social media. Everything that you know has taken the place of God in your life. If you're triggered – I am speaking to you. It often means that life on the outside as we know it tends to move on without us, people make progress, become booked & busy as well as start talking about us wondering why we appear to be making no progress while we seem to be in this stagnant place of waiting on God without a defined time frame. At least if we knew how long this process was going to take – it would be much easier to trust right? Well, it actually wouldn't be called trust or Faith if you had everything figured out. In fact, *"without faith it is impossible to please Him" (Hebrews 11:6).*

Waiting on God while He is working on you is NEVER a waste of time. How can waiting on the Redeemer of time be a waste of time? You will not miss out! Trying to keep it moving without Him is the real waste of time and you will always find yourself back to square one as there are levels you will never reach until the state of your heart is dealt with in God's presence. There are levels you will never reach until your pride, desires, rebellion, insecurities, character, fantasies, secret thought life & other things are sorted out by the Holy Spirit. There are no shortcuts with God.

I didn't take time to wait – was it then a surprise that I internally crashed the moment my sin came to light? Those who won't be crushed will inevitable one day crash. I didn't have the peace OF God which is a fruit that is produced as you walk daily with the Holy Spirit. I didn't take a step back and retreat into the presence of the Lord so He could really empty everything inside of it that was not like Him. I was okay to keep it moving according to my own definition of what moving on was.

Don't get me wrong, I am not saying that had I repented the right way initially then the pill would have worked. Oh no! Please don't for a moment entertain that thought! Again, that is a prime example of irresponsible Christianity and the idea that we can somehow twist God's arm into doing what we want Him to do. The only way to prevent an unplanned pregnancy would have been to keep my legs firmly closed. Period. As I said earlier, God is not a genie or a fairy godmother. Consequences will always be consequences – they have their place in all of our lives. Rightfully so. What I am saying is that I would have been able to navigate my pregnancy with a greater level of strength, soundness of mind and sureness that everything was going to work out for my good because I had God with me in spite of it all. We must aim to reach a level of spiritual maturity in God that sees God as good not just because He has helped us escape trouble but because He has preserved us even in the midst of trouble.

I would have still been able to build and maintain a strong relationship with God and an assurance of the outcome of my future whether it would take 1 year, 5 years or 10 years. I wouldn't have lived in fear and I certainly would not have succumbed to the overwhelming sense of condemnation that I carried with me everywhere that I went.

In Psalm 51:6-12 David prayed what I deem to be one of the most profound prayers ever prayed and it shows us perfectly what our posture should be when we say we are repenting for our sins before God:

"Behold, You desire ***truth in the inward parts,*** *And in the hidden part You will make me to know wisdom.* ***Purge me*** *with hyssop, and I shall be clean; Wash me, and I shall be whiter than snow. Make me hear joy and gladness, That the bones You have broken may rejoice. Hide Your face from my sins and blot out all my iniquities.* ***Create in me a clean heart,*** *O God, And* ***renew a steadfast spirit*** *within me. Do not cast me away from Your presence, And do not take Your Holy Spirit from me.* ***Restore to me the joy of Your salvation*** *and uphold me by Your generous Spirit."*

Take a moment to meditate on the words that are in bold. Do they sound like things that happen after a 5-minute prayer telling God you are sorry? Forgiveness is instant – yes but God's dealings, workings and fixing of the state of your heart are not. The Bible reminds us: *"The heart of man is desperately deceitful above all things and desperately wicked. Who can know it?" (Jeremiah 17:9).* Only God can handle the human heart.

Look at it this way: If I run the tap in my kitchen right NOW - I know for a fact that clean water will come out of it & I can drink it with absolutely no problems whatsoever. Agreed? Agreed. However, if I take that same clean, drinkable water from my kitchen tap & go through the extra step of putting it through a water filter – I will be most surprised to see the impurities that will suddenly be revealed in the water we have just agreed is perfectly okay for me to drink simply because these impurities were hidden from my naked eye. However, their hidden state did not reduce their very present state. Therefore, we can safely conclude that there must be a difference between that which is clean & that which is pure.

When we don't press deep into the presence of the Lord – we miss out on him revealing things about us that are hidden to the naked eye. Hidden. But. Present. Things that we would have otherwise never known. Things our own vision could never see. Things that may explain why we have been going around in circles for so long. Things that will reveal the root of some of the unpleasant fruit we see displayed in our lives. Things that will bring crystal clarity as to why there seems to still be something amiss in our lives though we go to church & tick all of the so called "Child of God" boxes. Things that separate the clean from the pure. Invisible does not necessarily mean Non-Existent. Functionality does not necessarily equate to Approved by God. God's love for you does not necessarily mean that He is pleased with you. Clean hands are one thing. Pure hearts are the goal. Hygiene is another thing. Holiness is the ultimate goal.

Do you see why genuine repentance is so important in the life of anyone who claims to be a Christian? Do you see how it is for your good & actually to protect you? Do you also see that it cannot be a one off or an event-based thing like I did at that conference? We must constantly allow the Holy Spirit to check our hearts. Sin is always a heart issue and not about whatever part of your body that has finally committed the act be it your eye, mouth or hands. Before my legs opened physically, they had opened in my heart. The complexity of your heart requires time and consistency at His feet allowing Him to have His way within you. You will be surprised to discover who you really are and what is truly buried on the inside of you if you spend enough time with God.

He desires truth from our inside parts of us. It is possible for us to say one thing with our lips & not mean it at all. We can wear a mask on the outside, have a certain way we present ourselves to people and a persona that is loved and admired by many. God is not moved by all of that. 1 Samuel 16:7 says, *"But the Lord said to Samuel do not look at his appearance or at his physical stature, because I have refused him. For the Lord does not see as man sees; for man looks at the outward appearance, but the Lord looks at the heart."* It is important to be honest about how you ended up in a situation in the first place & allow the Spirit of God to convict you. Most people think they fornicated because they ended up in the same bed with someone. Although factual, that's not the truth about the situation. Remember God desires truth not just facts. We must always take time to allow the Holy Spirit to search us. After all, He is the One that leads us into all truth so how else can I come to a revelation about the truth of a matter if I don't spend deliberate time with Him?

I didn't fornicate because I ended up in a room alone with him. I fornicated because I allowed boundaries to be broken. Boundaries were broken because in the most crucial decision-making moment my flesh was stronger than my Spirit. My flesh was stronger than my spirit because for a while especially leading up to that particular conference, that is what I had been feeding more. In the lift on the way to the room I could feel the Holy Spirt tugging at my heart strings and warning me – I ignored.

In fact, it had been a big drama (financially) for me to even attend the weekend in the first place and I vividly remember eventually having to borrow money to attend that weekend – money I struggled to pay back. All the while I ignored the still small voice that was trying to tell me that all of the confusion involved in arranging what would have usually been such a simple and straightforward trip was the Holy Spirit telling me not to go. He was warning me away from yes even a church gathering. I fornicated because I ignored the Holy Spirit from the very onset. I ignored Him. I grieved Him.

Ignoring someone who you have been in a lengthy love relationship with is not something that happens overnight. It happens little by little. I ignored Him because I had been listening to my own desires. He got replaced by him & for a season my then boyfriend had become my god and the object of my worship. I moved quicker for him if he requested something than I did for the Lord when He asked me to come and spend time with Him. The Shammah who would pray first before phoning any human being about ANYTHING disappeared. Ministry became a routine and I stopped operating from the presence of God and allowed the gift to carry me from ministration to ministration in the same way that a kite will effortlessly glide through the air because of the wind. I didn't fall into sin. I walked towards sin – we both did & met each other there.

If you honestly trace your steps back you will see where your relationship with the Lord started to get weaker. The notion that you just "found yourself" in sin is not true. It is never true. There is always a starting point. Get honest. It's either you were never truly living for God in the first place or you were & you started to let the standard slip somewhere along the way. For me the standard slipped massively & things went from holy to sinful repeatedly behind closed doors.

Maybe you started skipping some prayer time. I did. Maybe you began shortening your quiet time in a hurry to do other things. I did. Perhaps you began spending more and more time on social media. I did. Or around the wrong crowds or watching garbage on TV or entertaining ungodly conversations on the phone. Maybe you entered into a relationship you shouldn't have but you were so tired of being lonely you ignored that conviction to immediately u-turn. Or your heart got broken and instead of taking the pain and grief to the feet of Jesus – you started looking elsewhere for comfort and a way to cope. Whatever it was, it caused your heart to slowly get cold towards the Lord. If you are a genuine Child of God there is always a starting point for the deterioration of your relationship with Him. Such a level of honesty and transparency within yourself and towards God will bring true healing to your life & help prevent sin from becoming a repeated cycle.

Speaking of transparency, I don't know why we have such a difficult time being transparent before God as Christians. One thing that has to stop immediately is our shameless hiding behind prayers such as *"Lord I confess every known and unknown sin in Jesus name. Amen"* before quickly rushing off to the next prayer point. "Known & unknown!?" When I was fornicating, I knew exactly what I was doing so how dare I go before the King of Kings and merely label it *"a known or unknown sin?"* Every position, every sound and every word I knew & willingly orchestrated so why would I hide now? Why suddenly care about my dignity when I didn't care as I spread my legs akimbo? Do we actually have reverence for God or we take His love for granted? What I can't confess will always control me. It was called fornication and my prayer had to be: *"Lord forgive me for fornicating and having sex outside of marriage. Forgive me for ignoring your voice & choosing my flesh over you. I desecrated your temple. I am sorry etc..."* HUMILITY! While there are some things we do wrong unknowingly which do fall under that category / a LOT we know the exact name and title of. Call it what it is!

I am sure that on at least one occasion you have had people who have wronged you approach you with: *"If I offended you, then I am sorry" or "Sorry for whatever I did"* as though they can't for a moment pause, reflect & put their brain cells together to figure out clearly what they did wrong. Such side eye worthy behaviour. We all agree that it is an insult of the highest kind especially from someone who claims to love you and 9 out of 10 times the conversation has not ended well as offence takes hold of the steering wheel. So why offer that to the Lord? Call it out for what it is so that it finally loses its grip on your life.

By the time sin manifests it will have been encouraged by disobedience to the often still small voice of the Lord. A little compromise here, a spoonful of prayerlessness there, a dash of people pleasing here & a sprinkle of being distracted from your daily devotion time there. You hear Him calling and tugging at your heart but you ignore. You must humble yourself. Identify where it all went wrong or where it usually goes wrong for you. There is always a starting point. Blaming the devil is not good enough because without an access point in the first place he cannot wreak havoc in your life. Remember I said if he is in, it's because you allowed him in. Even he has to abide by spiritual laws & principles which require your cooperation whether on purpose or by omission for him to throw a party in your life.

As one who grew up in the church as well as being a minister, I have seen many Pastors, leaders & people who are supposed to lead an exemplary life fall into sin over the years. Too many to count. Unsurprisingly, the news of their scandal tends to spread like wildfire across social media, the newspapers, TV and in people's households across the world. Their social media followings double or triple overnight and DMs definitely start popping as Christians book their front row seat to receive the latest updates about said Man or Woman of God's life and above all observe if they will ever make a "comeback" from their humiliation. The difference between those who genuinely recover and get restored (by God not man) after a fall & those whose lives are visibly never quite the same or who walk away from God altogether is found in the approach they have when it comes to repentance.

Many Christians seem to think it is "religious" to take some time out of public ministry to spend time with the Lord behind closed doors after they sin. I've heard my fellow ministers say one too many times *"I've already repented before God. I don't need to keep doing it. I've been forgiven. I have to keep it moving."* Well, they are right. They have been forgiven but remember repentance is in two parts.

They feel that for some reason they will be putting more attention on their sin and not embracing the "full benefits" of the Cross by simply taking extra time out to spend with the Lover whose heart they broke in the first place. They forget it's a relationship. They also forget that everything we do publicly as children of God is supposed to be an overflow of private intimacy and not the other way around. *"all my springs are in you" (Psalms 87:7).* For most, they believe that the quicker they get back onto the stage and into the limelight before the people of God the quicker people will realise that God has indeed forgiven them and that they have 'moved on.' It is more about sending a strong message to the people of God to "keep it moving" onto the next piece of hot news than it is about the restorative power of God being genuinely displayed in and through their life in God's way and God's timing and for God's glory. It's about being restored back to everything and everyone else but God. The root of this is pride. Anyone who would rather prove their title, credibility or status before man instead of humbling themselves before God in secret and falling deeper in love with God where there are no lights, camera or audience is more lost than they know.

The passing of time is not automatic freedom from guilt, shame and condemnation. They can still hang over you and around you like a fly that just won't go away. It is the devil's job to accuse you daily as often as he can in every way he can. "*Then I heard a loud voice saying in heaven, "Now salvation, and strength, and the kingdom of our God, and the power of His Christ have come, for the accuser of our brethren, who accused them before our God day and night, has been cast down" (Revelations 12:10).* Some of your frustrations, jealousies, lashing out & issues that you have with OTHER people are down to the load of guilt that you are secretly carrying. You haven't allowed God to deal with you and so you take it out on other people such as spouse, your children, your relatives, your friends or strangers on social media.

If the truth is to be told, THEY are not your problem. You have a problem with YOURSELF. What is haunting you is unconfessed sin. What is haunting you is your refusal to spend quality time at the feet of Jesus being built back up again. It bothers us to see the glory of God upon a life that was once a mess and sight of shame not knowing that the same is available for us if only we would correct our postures. For how long will another persons smile, progress, restoration & success eat away at you in secret as you scroll social media because you truly long for the same but have not submitted yourself in the presence of the Only one who can bring about the same in your own life? Repent!

There's a way one walks when carrying a bag that is too heavy for them & so just because you can still walk doesn't mean you're walking right. Functionality doesn't necessarily equate wholeness & unfortunately in this day and age it's used as a mask to hide what is really taking place beneath the surface. Is it not wise to be strengthened, restored & healed in the secret place even if it means months of silence as God works on you?

Repentance done right is what brings about true freedom. Repentance done right is what brings healing to your life. Repentance done right gives you strength in the face of the people in the midst of their judgement against you. Repentance done right is what lifts that heavy weight off your chest. Repentance done right is what enables you to smile & laugh genuinely without it being a cover for secret pain. Repentance done right will do away with all of those social media proving-a-point to people tendencies. Repentance done right evicts shame from your identity. Repentance done right will take away your need to dress seductively to draw attention to yourself unnecessarily. Repentance done right is what frees you from the need to compare yourself to others. Repentance done right is the key to everything you are so desperately looking for.

Don't rush to prove a point to anyone. People in a rush are the ones whose so called "comebacks" lack longevity, whose ministries begin to lose effectiveness and purity or those who start being obsessed with talking about haters in every single thing that they do because they have now become paranoid. Sin makes you weak, fearful, ashamed and timid. It produces nothing but death. *"For the wages of sin is death, but the gift of God is eternal life in Christ Jesus our Lord" (Romans 6:23.)*

Many will create a false strong personality to deceive the masses & to prove yet another point that they are okay but the inside of their heart and mind tell a completely different story. Many will rush to post belly pictures and videos of them oh so happy and unbothered so they can control the narrative of their sin but it is nothing but an attempt to deceive. It is so much hard work to pretend you are strong every single day of your life when you can get true strength from waiting on God. Why pretend when it can be your reality if you would just take some time to be with the Lord? When did quality time in the presence of God become a punishment? Why rush to impress people who will immediately forget about you at the next piece of fresh gossip when there is One who calls you the *"apple of His eye"* in Zechariah 2:8 and One before whom who you will always matter for the right reasons? Is He not more important? Instead of trying to silence the people talk to God. As you talk to God, He will silence anything that needs silencing starting with the storm raging on the inside of you.

My generation would rather offer God flowers of public service for the likes and shares than true secret place intimacy that gets no applause from man but pleases the heart of God. Similar to a husband who beats his wife mercilessly and apologises in every possible way except a changed heart. Their itineraries and schedules become more filled than they were prior to their fall but their private devotion time slacks and declines. Their social media becomes filled with activity, videos, quotes and noise in the name of Jesus while their Bibles gather dust at home. Is it a wonder then that: *"Many will say to Me in that day, 'Lord, Lord, have we not prophesied in Your name, cast out demons in Your name, and done many wonders in Your name?' And then I will declare to them, 'I never knew you; depart from Me, you who practice lawlessness!" (Matthew 7:22-23).* Please hear me! It is not religious to choose to go deeper in God and with God by taking time OUT from life as usual after you have fallen. It is not a lack of faith in your Heavenly Father's forgiveness towards you. It is a display of love. An understanding that you never want anything to come between the two of you again and so you are going to eliminate all gaps between you, work it out and walk hand in hand with Him again. That ability to feel. Now that is love.

The reason I felt like I had to re-repent was because I didn't immerse myself in the presence of God to the depth I should have done after falling not realising that a storm was around the corner and I needed to be able to stand firm in it. And even if by some chance I hadn't gotten pregnant, His presence should have still been a priority. Getting pregnant forced me to confront and see some things that I may have still been ignoring and blinded to up until this day. Seeking Him for more than what He can do for me or give me should have been a priority. Seeking His face should have been a priority.

How I wish I had neglected my mobile phone, food, Netflix and social media, my boyfriend and everything else that I deemed to be more important than Abba in that season for some extra shut away time with Him in my bedroom seeking His face and resting in Him.

That way when my titles of Minister, Mentor, Preacher & Worship Leader came to the forefront of my mind and how much of a disappointment I now was to the Body of Christ I could boldly remind the enemy that I was forgiven, and that God still had a plan for me. I would have reminded the enemy that the greatest title I could ever hold was CHILD OF GOD & that I was a son before I had ever been sent.

That way when I caught people nudging elbows as I entered a room with my undeniable bump I could have internal peace knowing that their opinions did not define me but the God I had sought and was still seeking in secret had the final say over my life. That way when I went to crowded places I would not have needed to silently beg God that I didn't see anyone who knew who I was. I would have walked with an unshakeable calmness in my soul. That way I would have had the strength to pray and rebuke the enemy from my dream life as night after night I was chased, harassed, attacked & choked and more. That way when I scrolled social media and saw other female ministers on fire for Jesus, doing exploits for the Kingdom of God I would not have been overwhelmed with discouragement, quiet jealousy, the spirit of comparison and feelings of being a hopeless case. I would have remembered that the God who was using them was *still* able to use me for His glory as well.

That way when the slaps, pokes, kicks and physical abuse happened the first time, it would have also been the last time because the notion that I somehow deserved it would have had no runway to land in my soul. That way when thoughts, suggestions and pressures to *abort* in order to save our reputation and image in the eyes of man came pounding on the doorstep of my convictions I would not for a moment have considered it, even slightly. That way, suicide would never have even momentarily seemed like a more preferable option because I would have been sure without a shadow of a doubt that because He lives I could still face tomorrow.

How I wish I had *truly* repented.

----- CHAPTER THREE -----

TWO WRONGS DON'T MAKE A RIGHT

"I wish you could make IT disappear. Kill IT. You should get rid of IT. Nobody should find out about this!" The young lady read the text messages that she couldn't bring herself to delete and replayed the various phone conversations in her mind over and over again & sobbed violently on her bed. A pain she will probably never be able to adequately describe gushed through her body as she wrestled with her conscience. It didn't appear like she was winning.

She didn't want to kill her baby. She knew better than that. She knew God more than that. She knew that two wrongs had never in the history of man or the standard of God made a right yet here she was being pressured to commit a wrong – and actually beginning to consider it. She struggled for breath as her nostrils blocked due to the intensity of her anguish.

Days passed as she wrestled with what her final decision was going to be.

"Don't kill it sis. Everything will be alright"

"Don't kill it. That pressure is wrong. It is the devil."

"No one is killing any baby if I have anything to do with it sis!" She meditated on the advice some of her older sisters had given her as she confided in them about the mounting pressure to abort. It all sounded right but she didn't think she had enough strength for that road.

Yes. She was going to do it. As her hands shook, she opened Google on her phone and began to search where in her area she could have an abortion done. She waited for the page to load.

No! She couldn't. She knew better, come on! She felt the tears increase in speed as they fell down the sides of her face. What could she do though? What options did she have? Support hadn't come from where it should have. Maybe this was the best way. Maybe it was the wisest decision, after all she was a public figure and she couldn't handle the accusation that kept replaying in her mind that she had deliberately ruined someone else's reputation. The page continued to load. Yes. She had to do it. Soon she would know where to go to do what she thought she needed to do.

"Call Aunty!" The girl paused and wondered who had made that suggestion. It was only her in the room and it had not been an audible voice but she knew that someone had spoken and was leading her to call her Aunty in that very moment. Immediately.. An Aunty she had not spoken to in almost forever. Wouldn't that be awkward though? And why her? I mean… She stopped her thoughts and picked up her phone. She was already confused and bewildered and so instead of trying to make sense of the supernatural urge she simply obeyed. For the first time in a long time she obeyed.

"Hello my baby! How are you?" That joy in Aunty's voice had always been her trademark. Unfortunately, today the young lady could not reciprocate. Instead the words flowed out of her like water before she had a moment to think about what she was saying.

"Aunty… I'm pregnant. I'm being pressured to kill my baby! Please help me!"

As I write, my beautiful daughter is currently having her afternoon nap. I did, however, have to pause just now to offer worship to God as tears of inexplicable gratitude filled my eyes. Such a response has become a regular occurrence when I take a look at the immense bundle of joy my daughter is. If you have ever met Tiiana Anashe then you know she is an entire mood! She is indeed such a gift and it still seems like a dream to me that I came so close to committing the unthinkable as I reached breaking point within myself. I didn't deserve it but out of His loving kindness and tender mercies somehow and some way God made a way for me to be able to do the right thing in the face of my wrong. I know that the stories of many others have not ended quite so fortunately and for that I will always be grateful. For sure, the following Scripture came alive for me on that precious day: *"No temptation has overtaken you except such as is common to man; but God is faithful, who will not allow you to be tempted beyond what you are able, but with temptation will also make the way of escape, that you may be able to bear it" (1 Corinthians 10:13).*

Obeying the instruction to call my Aunty was my beautiful way of escape and she immediately began ministering to me as I wept on the phone, reminding me that God was not done with me and He also had a plan for the baby I was carrying. I can clearly remember how such a bold, authoritative but loving tone suddenly came over her voice as she concluded with telling me, *"DO NOT KILL THAT BABY!"*

A wave of internal strength swept me and it was like scales suddenly fell from my eyes. Ehh? Kill who? How? And why?I woke up! I ferociously determined within me that no matter what lay ahead of me I was going to keep my baby even if it meant facing the world alone. She took such a bold charge of the situation and sounded the alarm by calling my parents (who I was completely terrified to ring myself) and immediately ensuring that people who truly feared God and who could simultaneously focus on all of the major issues in the whole situation: my relationship with God, my well being and the baby's well being, came into the know about my secret. The enemy's suggestions no longer had anywhere to hide & I could receive daily encouragement and strength from stronger Christians. That day, the enemy lost a big battle as light overcame darkness and as I watch my daughter grow I have been given another reason ontop of the many that already existed to worship the One & Only Living God: Jesus.

I cannot imagine my life without my daughter and to think that the enemy would have had me miss out on the privilege that it is to raise her is one of the things that makes me more determined every day to live in a way that glorifies God and bring utter terror to his camp. Motherhood is a calling and it is an assignment to raise a generation that will go on to fearlessly advance the Kingdom of God. A generation that fears God. Satan was really determined to utterly destroy my destiny but mercy said NO.

Two wrongs don't make a right. I am sure you have heard that statement more times than you can count & again today I remind you of this with every fibre of my being. It does not matter what has happened and it doesn't matter how dark things look, it is always better to walk through the consequences of your action than to try and somehow rescue yourself out of the situation by playing God. I have already talked about the distance from God and the horror it is to live a life separated from Him but do you know that onto of that you put your own life at risk when you decide that you will have an abortion? Do you know that you can die? Do you know that you can potentially never have children again in your life? All for what? A reputation?

The main thing that lies behind our desire to cover up our sin is the fear of what people will have to say when they find out about what we have done. Fear of people. We would rather avoid being talked about, labelled by our wrong & rejected by those who know us at all cost instead of doing the right thing. *"And do not fear those who kill the body but cannot kill the soul. But rather fear Him who is able to destroy both soul and body in hell" (Matthew 10:28).*

Make or break moments like this in life truly reveal who we have made the source of our identity. They expose who we really are and whose we really are. There is no such thing as "this situation left me without any choice – I wouldn't normally have done this." That is a lie. The Word of God warns us to *"Keep your heart with all diligence, For out of it spring the issues of life" (Proverbs 4:23).* One of my fathers in the Lord explained it to me this way: The reason a television responds to a remote control is not just because there are batteries in the remote but because there is also something inside the television that has been programmed to respond to the remote. It's a two-way thing. So, while the enemy is able to pile an indescribable amount of pressure on us – he needs something within us to work with. Whatever situations we find ourselves in always expose & reveal who we actually are and the parts of our flesh that are yet to be crucified with Christ. Remember what I said about the difference between clear water and pure water. If it comes out of you. It's in your heart.

If you truly lives as a Child of God, though the ultimate goal is to live a righteous life – even if you fall short of the mark, the way you deal with the fall should still be a reflection of who you are and who you belong to. Don't allow the enemy to lead you to adopt an identity that was nailed to the Cross thousands of years ago. He wants you to believe that you have messed up so badly 'already' so you may as well continue. Well, I remind you that Jesus died for you 'already' so you may as well stop.

As I made that Google search on my phone that evening I was slowly becoming convinced that this was the best solution as it would mean everything could just go back to normal as if nothing had happened. This 'solution' began to seem like just the perfect thing I needed to end all of my troubles and worries. It was a quick fix with lifelong consequences that the enemy momentarily but successfully convinced me I could always deal with at a later date.

In that moment I forgot about the One who bled and died on the Cross of Calvary for me so that I could approach Him without fear no matter what it is I had done. I momentarily forgot that on that day when the blood of Jesus gushed out of His body with every wound the soldiers inflicted on Him and every beating He took it was for the exact moment I would choose to become one with a man who was not my husband. The blood of Jesus was enough. The blood of Jesus is enough. For me and also for you.

The Bible says: *"The one who loves his life [eventually] loses it [through death], but the one who hates his life in this world [and is concerned with pleasing God] will keep it for life eternal" (John 13:25).* Sin masked as self-preservation is one of the most dangerous things that you can do and once you start it will be one thing after the other until a day of reckoning when you will look up and find yourself in a place so far away from God that you could have never dreamed possible. The devil is a master at convincing us that we only have one option to take when we find ourselves facing so much pressure and uncertainty. He magnifies our sin until all we can think about is finding an emergency exit from our reality at any possible cost. However, the sin you don't deal with today will be the sin that deals with you tomorrow.

I certainly felt like I was all out of options in that season because the only thing I could think of was abortion. There was no way out! However looking back now I now know that it is not every situation in life that you will always be able to find a way OUT of especially when you choose not take the initial way OUT of the temptation that preceded that situation. There are some situations that only have a way THROUGH them if we will surrender to God and go through them with God no matter how difficult, humiliating & challenging. I am reminded of the God who parted the Red Sea for the Israelites in the book of Exodus. Even though the Red Sea was not before them as a result of disobedience we see how He was able to take them from one end to the other. If you choose obedience even after your own disobedience – God will carry you through too.

In 2 Samuel 11 & 12 we read of the time when David attempted to use two wrongs to make a right. It goes without saying that he failed miserably. David committed adultery with a woman named Bathsheba and impregnated her in the process. She was another mans wife. Yup, a whole wife – imagine... He devised a plan that ensured her husband (a soldier in David's army) would be killed on the battlefield. That way he would never find out what David had done with his wife & David could go on to marry Bathsheba and have her as his own. Covetousness, lust, deception, murder, pride and adultery. Mys oh my, what a resumé of sins. The perfect cover up except that David forgot one minor MAJOR detail: God had seen and God knew. David paid direly for his sins. Open 2 Samuel 12:10-15 for yourself and have a read of the consequences of David's actions. They even effected generations to come!

Do you know that your actions today will ALSO affect generations to come after you? Sometimes we are so blinded into only seeing the now, feeling the now & acting based on the now that we forget to look at things from God's perspective as well as looking at the bigger picture. What will be said of your bloodline because of the decisions that you make today? What stories will your descendants have to tell of you because of the decisions you make today? If you don't care then you need to ask God to change your heart. Some of you have it so hard in life, finances, dreams at night, relationships & more because of some of the decisions, deals & covenants of your ancestors that you are currently having to fight your way through.

It is known in some bloodlines that all of the men step put on their wives at some point or father a child outside of their marriage covenant or that all of the men are alcoholics or women beaters. It is known in some bloodlines that all of the women can never get married or that they all suffer from the same sicknesses and illnesses. In other family's people die at the same age or are unable to do anything productive with their lives no matter how much money comes into their hands. Hear me well, for an evil altar to speak so strongly and continuously in a bloodline it was first given a voice through a decision to disobey God which in turn birthed a culture of disobedience and ultimately a curse. You owe it to your descendants to leave a godly legacy for them and give them a fighting chance in life.

When satan tempted Jesus in Matthew 4 he made sure to appeal to what appeared to be Jesus' immediate need, desires and cravings. Think about it, what does a person who has been fasting for 40 days, want more than anything in the world?

FOOD! However, Jesus did not take the bait and He overcame the devil with the truth of the Word of God. This isn't to say that Jesus did not want bread, in fact I'm sure He would have loved some but when what He wanted was presented to Him by the enemy and not God, He knew He had to love God more. It is not about the thing but about who it is that is presenting the thing. The reason we can overcome temptation today is because we have an example through the life of Jesus when He was on Earth. If he had even slightly succumbed to the enemy's tactic – what hope would we have? Each time the devil came at him with a suggestion, Jesus responded with "It is written" and He defeated him! Jesus didn't have a physical Bible in His hand, he quoted the Word that was in Him.

This is why it is important to read the Word of God in every single season. Emergency based Bible reading is as foolish as a soldier starting His training on the day of battle. What helps a soldier when dealing with an enemy isn't the fact that he is on the battlefield but more-so everyday he spent off the battlefield in preparation for that day and moment. The Word of God that you store and keep in you is what will naturally rise up and flow out of you in the season of testing. If it's not in you – chances are that you will fail.

Of course, I wanted my reputation, life and everything that I knew to remain intact but the enemies offer for me to attain all of this was to commit abortion. Murder. He had nothing else to offer but death. Death to me. Death to my child. Meanwhile His evil agenda would have lived on and continued to thrive. I then had to choose to love God more than what I wanted and honour Him though an easy fix was merely another secret sin away. Oh, the temptation! It all came down to: who did I love more?

The only thing that can right wrong and wash us of our sins is the blood of Jesus and when we ask God to wash us in it and forgive us of our sins.

"In Him we have redemption through His blood, the forgiveness of sins, according to the riches of His grace" (Ephesians 1:7).

"But if we walk in the light as He is in the light, we have fellowship with one another, and ***the blood of Jesus Christ*** *His Son* ***cleanses us from all sin****" (1 John 1:7).*

"But now in Christ Jesus you who once were far off ***have been brought near by the blood of Christ****" (Ephesians 2:13).*

"How much more shall ***the blood of Christ,*** *who through the eternal Spirit offered Himself without spot to God,* ***cleanse your conscience*** *from dead works to serve the living God?" (Hebrews 9:14).*

"Therefore, brethren, ***having boldness to enter*** *the Holiest by* ***the blood of Jesus****" (Hebrews 10:19).*

I remind you that there will always be that one option presented by the enemy AS WELL AS God's option. Two options. There are always two options. Don't deny the existence of God's option because it is uncomfortable. We often fail to see God's way because it involves the crushing of our ego and reputation as well as the exposing of what we have done for all to see. It is the one that seems the most unfair, humbling & difficult but it is also the only option that will reap wonderful eternal results. If we say we love Him – He has got to become more important to us than us and how we feel. John the Baptist put it this way in John 3:30, *"He must increase, but I must decrease."* I could have taken the enemies one option of aborting the baby and to this day absolutely no one – including you who is reading this book would have ever known I fell pregnant out of wedlock. Think about how beautifully & peacefully wicked that sounds. Unknown to everyone but me, him & God. Oh, and the devil. And my dream life at night. And my health. And my future attempts at having children. And my peace of mind. And the innocent blood shed. And my random outbursts of guilt. Just "us" though. One big happy family.

Do you see how I had to choose to honour God? A choice. The very thought terrified me if I am to be honest. An anxiety drummed away daily in the very pits of my stomach unsure of what each day had in store for me even though I knew what the right decision was. However, the God I had encountered many times before and whose presence had always been a safe refuge for my heart, body & soul was now waiting for me to make a choice. I couldn't deny that I had once walked so tangibly with Him and witnessed His ability to walk me through the storm and nothing would break His heart more than me sinning AGAIN to cover something that had already broken His heart into a million pieces. While the wisdom of the world encouraged me to look out for my self (however temporary) & continue to maintain an image before you all in order to continue to be accepted by the world – God was requiring something more from me. He always requires something more. The wisdom of God is quite the opposite as it compels us to honour God even at the very cost of our status, following & perfect standing with man. It will allow us to be broken so God can build us back up again as He sees fit. *"For the wisdom of this world is foolishness with God. For it is written, "He catches the wise in their own craftiness." (1*

Corinthians 3:19). This is because God is more concerned about our spiritual growth over our comfort. Our souls over our feelings. Our eternal destination over our earthly standing with man.

The Bible says: *"For what will it profit a man if he gains the whole world, and loses his own soul? For whoever is ashamed of Me and My words in this adulterous and sinful generation, of him the Son of Man also will be ashamed when He comes in the glory of His Father with the holy angels" (Mark 8:36 & 38).* The opinions of your family, friends & followers are NOT worth it if it means you will compromise your relationship with God. Again, this is not something that is widely taught but it is the truth and it applies in every area of life. God must always come first. Don't justify it. It will never be right.

Allowing God to turn situations around for our good through humility and submission to His Word is how we come out victorious and with true testimonies that go on to transform lives. The Bible promises us the following: *"And we know that all things work together for good to those who love God, to those who are called according to His purpose" (Romans 8:28).* Things always turn out well for those who love God. Those who love God are not the ones who look presentable before man or who attend church on all 52 Sundays of the year. A perfected exterior while your insides are slowly rotting away has never impressed God. Those who love God are the ones who obey Him even when it costs them everything. *"if you love Me, keep My commandments" (John 14:15).*

This does not mean that you will not cry, you will but He will dry your tears. That's things working together for good. You will be talked about, but He will comfort you. That's things working together for good. They will write you off for good but

He will restore you stronger than ever before. That's things working together for good. They will call you names but He will give you a new name if you call on His name. That's things working out for your good. They will walk away from you but God will show you that He has always been more than enough for you anyway. That's things working out for your good. The bad will come and break you down but ultimately the goodness of God will triumph and He will give you beauty for ashes – if you stay the course. No shortcuts. No self. Just your hand in His completely.

Obedience in the seemingly impossible situations is how people like me get to have special moments when they can pause mid-writing while sitting on a stool on their kitchen table with a colourful bonnet on their head & look back at their journey & genuinely smile through tears of worship and gratitude to the Lord. Obedience is how your ears will reach a place where they no longer hear the voices of those who have vowed to never let you forget your sin. Instead they forever hear the voice of Abba day in and day out saying: *"Therefore, if anyone is in Christ, he is a new creation; old things have passed away; behold, all things have become new" (2 Corinthians 5:17).* Obedience is how your heart is filled with compassion for the very ones who hate the restoration God has done in you because the new heart that God has given you is able to discern that beneath the hate and the shade is a girl or a guy who is hiding horrible secrets of their own and desperately needs to be shown that guilt, shame & condemnation can loose their grip over them too. Obedience is also how Jesus came to be given the most powerful name that has ever existed. *"And being found in appearance as a man, He humbled Himself and became obedient to the point of death, even the death of the cross. Therefore, God also has highly exalted Him and given Him the name which is above every name" (Philippians 2:8-9)*. The name that when it is called upon, things that cannot be fathomed or imagined begin to take place.

Obey even when it is not convenient. Obey when it hurts. Obey when you know that they will laugh at you. Obey even when you don't have the full terminology to explain your decision to them. Obey when you know you will lose everything. Obey when you know you will be left alone with God. Obey.

There is no situation that will last forever neither have I ever seen anyone who chose God over man (especially themselves) and lived to regret it. Impossible. The Word of God says: *"Indeed, none of those who [expectantly] wait for You will be ashamed; Those who turn away from what is right and deal treacherously without cause will be ashamed (humiliated, embarrassed)" (Psalm 25:3 AMP).* That is a PROMISE! You can change the course of your destiny either by aligning yourself with God through obedience to His word or aligning yourself with the devil through disobedience to God. There are no special superpowers reserved for certain people so they find it easier than the rest of us to make godly decisions in their lives. If you have breath and a Bible you can win the battle against the enemy and step into obedience today.

Perhaps you are reading this & you have already used a wrong to try and right another wrong. Perhaps you have had an abortion and you're wondering where exactly you now fit into the equation. God is there for you too. He loves you. He loves you. He loves you. His love is greater than all the guilt, shame and condemnation that you may be feeling and He still wants you from the crown of your head to the souls of your feet. This is God's word to you today:

"The LORD has appeared of old to me, saying: "Yes, ***I have loved you with an everlasting love****; Therefore, with lovingkindness I have drawn you. Again,* ***I will build you, and you shall be rebuilt****, O virgin of Israel!* ***You shall again be adorned*** *with your tambourines and shall go forth in the dances of those who rejoice" (Jeremiah 31:3-4).*

Read it again. God is extremely in love with you without condition and if you apply all of the principles that I have listed from the start of this book e.g; humility, responsibility, repentance and simply sitting at the feet of Jesus unmoving like Mary in Luke 10 then your life can change too. While her sister Martha bused herself with all of the things she thought would please Jesus and impress him, Jesus' response to her was: *"Martha, Martha, you are worried and troubled about many things. But one thing is needed, and Mary has chosen that good part, which will not be taken away from her" (Luke 10:41-42).* The good part according to Him was simply getting close to Him and becoming still in His presence. Having one focus and agenda: Him.

The blood that was shed on the Cross was also for you. He will forgive you of your sins and yes even the fact that you may have shed innocent blood You are not excluded. You are not beyond redemption. You are not too far gone. You are not a hopeless case. Your family might have led you to believe that you are. They lied. Your church might have led you to believe that you are. They also lied. They may have gathered around you in a large circle ready and eagerly waiting to stone you and see you gone for good just like they did with that woman caught in adultery. Just like they did with me. But there is One whose only response to those who are listing your sins is:

"Whoever has no sin between all of you gathered here today - let them throw the first stone at her" (John 8:7).

God does not throw stones at you. He is love & He is waiting to restore you & give you true beauty for the ashes you have been walking around with. Will you choose Him today? Now…? He is a prayer away and has always been a prayer away. You don't have to go on a 3-day trek to find Him. Simply turn. The same way you would turn immediately in a crowded mall if you heard someone call your name aloud. Turn because He calls your name. Turn because after searching high and low it is safe to conclude that God is your only way out of the pain, the brokenness and the mess. Turn because He loves you.

Dear Lord, I pray for my friend who is reading this book right now. I thank you for the immense and immeasurable amount of love that you have for them. You know them inside out and you still love them. I stand in the gap for them as they read this. You are the only One who knows exactly what it is that burdens and pains their heart. You know it all. I ask that you release your strength over them now in the name of Jesus. Your strength is perfected in weakness- they need you now God. The devil has waged such a fierce war and without your divine intervention they will be completely consumed. As they pray with their own mouth in a moment after reading this prayer – may your Holy Spirit help them to be transparent before you. May you remind them that You are worth it. You are worth the humility. The brokenness. The heartfelt repentance. They don't have to be afraid. They can choose you and see the decision all of the way through no matter what comes their way because you promised to never leave nor forsake them. You promised to forgive any and all who would humbly come and ask you. May this be the moment something awakens within them in a way that cannot be influenced by anyone other than your Holy Spirit. In Jesus name I pray, Amen.

Your turn.

----- CHAPTER FOUR -----

SPREAD LIKE WILDFIRE

"Pastor, I'm pregnant with his baby. I need you to help us. I need advice. Can you talk to him please…?"

The young lady proceeded to pour out the contents of her heart and update the man of God about the predicament she was currently facing. She had already decided she was not going to abort her baby but as expected the strain of the unplanned pregnancy had began causing ever increasing tension and frustration in her relationship.

"…Hmm, tell me more…" The Pastor encouraged her ever so slyly.

The young lady continued, feeling the weight on her chest get lighter and lighter the more details she willingly let out of her system. Discernment, however, was screaming frantically at her that she should keep her mouth closed. That she was confiding in the wrong person. That she may as well have done an interview with the national news and screamed her secret for all to hear. That this was the last person she should be opening up to. She heard nothing. Discernment was on mute.

All the young lady could see was his title: PASTOR. Surely to be trusted, respected and admired? A shepherd of the sheep and while she was a leader herself she was severely bleeding and in need of tender loving care. And so, she carried on and on and on, spilling all. Every last detail.

She breathed a sigh of relief as the talk came to an end and reassurances that he would handle the matter calmed her mind. She went downstairs to try and eat something though the nausea had waged a fierce war against her. She had sent messages to another man of God in desperation. A "father" but in spectacular blue tick fashion he had not responded. He never did.

The young lady was completely oblivious however, that as she ate, feeling somewhat more peaceful… all across the country and across the globe, minute by minute, from household to household, phone to phone and certainly DM to DM they had just become the latest hot topic.

It was indeed a Pastor who first spread the news of my pregnancy to some of the masses like wildfire long before we were ready to share it with the world. I had called the Pastor because the level of disagreement & strife in my relationship was becoming unbearable for me to handle. Everything was a vicious argument or fight via the phone. I decided that we needed help. At this point morning sickness had taken its full effect on me & I was unable to keep anything, including water, down. I also contracted E. coli during my first trimester which is bacteria infection that causes severe abdominal cramps, bloody diarrhoea, nausea and constant fatigue.

I kept being told *"These are just pregnancy symptoms", "It's normal, you have to get up and move girl", "Pregnancy is not a disease. Don't baby yourself"* and more until I dragged myself to the doctors to find out what was truly wrong with me. It turned out it was a lot more than just ordinary pregnancy. I was put on a course of antibiotics and just as I was recovering I contracted E. coli again. It was so horrible! I laid in bed for weeks unable to do anything and feeling very sorry for myself. All of this physical, emotional & mental toll weeks into the pregnancy was proving too much for me to bare. I rang him because I knew the two of them to be somewhat friends who confided in each-other from time to time. This Pastor came across as someone so trustworthy, welcoming and highly concerned about his well being and so I thought who better to *"knock sense into him"* man to man? Big mistake.

Please understand that not everyone can be trusted with your mess, even if they hold a spiritual title and I learnt that the very hard way. You need to share whatever it is you need to share with wisdom so that you actually receive the godly help that you need and not an exposure to more shame. The Bible says in Proverbs 13:3, *"He who guards his mouth preserves his life,*

But he who opens wide his lips shall have destruction." You can avoid a lot by simply keeping your mouth quiet and waiting to open it at the right place, at the right time & in the right way. Growing up my Mum would always say, "silence cannot be quoted"

If it is true help that you are looking for then tread with wise caution and spirit led caution – if it's simply attention that you seek: do as you please. Just because they are willing to listen does not mean that they should be told. Just because they are willing to advise does not mean they should be trusted. Just because they are available does not mean they have the capacity to handle what you desire to share. Titles are meaningless in the absence of godly character and sadly one too many people have tales to tell about the scars they have received as a result of those those in the church who were supposed to cover and protect them but instead brutally wounded them.

Is that how the Body of Christ is supposed to be though? Whatever happened to living by the Word of God: *"A new commandment I give to you, that you love one another; as I have loved you, that you also love one another" (John 13:34).* At what point did we become a people who will gather for the sole purpose of celebrating our fellow Believer's downfall? When did our tea & coffee start tasting sweeter if it is accompanied by the latest gossip of sister A or brother B? In which moment did the blood of Jesus become sufficient for our sins but not so much for those of our neighbour? When did Christ because our lawyer for life in the court room but a prosecutor for everyone else? When did Christian leaders become the people to be feared the most in terms of addressing and adequately dealing with the sins of those who they were called to cover with love?

To say I was angry and disappointed is an understatement. I was furious. As in pregnant Shammah furious.

But it was too late and to be honest I didn't have the time to do the usual confrontation I would have done with my *"how could you!"* type clap-back under any other circumstance. I had to take this L with my chest as painful as it was and as much as it further complicated things for me. I was simply too sick at the time to make his actions that much of a major focal point – there were better things to shed tears over. I had just set my mind on keeping my child and that was what I had to keep my mind on. I couldn't take back my phone call or reverse what he had done. I simply took it as a lesson to be more discerning in future and to always pour out my heart from a place of wisdom as well as divine direction and not a place of desperation. Even if I had somehow missed the lesson I was reminded over and over during the first half of my pregnancy: *"That will teach you not to open your mouth and talk to everyone Shammah."* Life had to move on.

I remember one of the main headlines in that season being the fact that I had previously and publicly said that I believed that Christian couples who are dating or courting should NOT kiss until their wedding day in order to avoid any and all temptation. My oh my did the saints have a field day with that one. My name was quickly forgotten and replaced with "Sister hypocrite" , "Minister double standard" as the obvious was pieced together: her now out of wedlock pregnancy had surely started with a KISS! True, it had. The same kiss I had told countless others to make sure to abstain from.

Had any one of them came to ask me to my face I would have shared with them that I failed God and I knew I had failed Him. I would have said I was sorry because I genuinely was. I would have told them that I became weak though I had made sure to wholeheartedly live right previously at some point before it all went horribly wrong. I would have shared that even though

I failed, I still believed in holiness and purity. That even though I had failed, I would still preach purity with all my strength because my falling short of the standard did not change that the standard was there and was never going to change. My failings did not change the Word of God. I would have asked for even the shortest prayer to be made on my behalf by them at any point during their mockery of me because a battle for not just my future but my very life raged day in and day out. I would have told them that if God could forgive them then He could surely forgive me. Nobody asked though.

I sincerely believe that our inability as a church to truly display the love of Christ is one of the reasons why the world does not take us seriously. How can it? There is nothing attractive about a people who will eagerly turn on and devour each-other like animals at the first given opportunity. The Bible makes a very clear statement that will forever ring true: *"And if a house is divided against itself, that house cannot stand" (Mark 3:25).* Instead of being a safe place for the confrontation of sin (yes covering does not mean leaving something unconfronted!), we are the last place people want to come to for help because our track record shows that we kick people down when they are already down. We wound the already wounded. We oppress the already oppressed. We violently hunt down those who have long waved the white flag of surrender in search for help. Ironically, all in the name of Jesus.

Just the other day as I scrolled social media I came across a Facebook post talking about how a well-known music minister had a sex tape of him indulging in homosexual activities that had just been leaked to the public by someone. Many comments caught my eyes as Christians begged for a link to be sent to them in their private inboxes so that they could watch the video for themselves. *Begging. To see* someone's sex tape. On a public post. That can be viewed by all. Viewed but the same colleagues, neighbours, mentees, friends and family who see you posting about God, your undying love for Him and all of His goodness. Are you surprised that they don't take you seriously when tomorrow you put back on the handmade Child of God hat on your head instead of the helmet of salvation that is supposed to be firmly fixed in place for life. No, really.

John 8 shows us another way. The only way. God's way. Instead of condemning the woman caught in adultery. He showed her mercy & love. She was guilty! She was wrong! She was an adulteress! Yes. Yes. Yes. And yet, Christ's love covered her in front of a crowd of people ready to rightfully kill her. Christ gave her a fresh and clean slate when the world was ready to write her off for good. This is our example. Our only example and also what should be our only option. To show love in everything that we do. To glorify and honour God in the way we deal with those who have fallen, even if they are supposed to *know better.* To wholeheartedly partner with God's ability to restore a fallen believer stronger and better than before they fell so that God's name may be glorified.

To condemn another human being is to forget that you yourself have been forgiven of the unforgiveable by God. To condemn someone is to commit the sin of believing that your sins are in any way better than those of another person. To condemn someone is to forget the many secret sins you have in your closet that have never been exposed and just how easily tables could turn. A secret sin of masturbation or watching of pornography is no better than someone who has their fornication tape leaked to the public. Both are sinners. To condemn someone is to forget that the blood of Jesus is enough for you, me and them.

Sadly, and often times, people are in hidden competition and comparison with those who have fallen and so news of that latest scandal is a huge sigh of relief for them. They feel that their neighbour's shame somehow immediately promotes them and puts them in a more favourable light with the people and with the Lord. That is the problem with living for the gram instead of living for God. They feel their neighbours fall makes their own reputation climb up in the "polls" and they become more likeable in comparison to their fellow fallen brethren. However, the aim of this life is not to be pleasing before man – it is to remain upright and pleasing before God. Proverbs 17*:5* AMP *says, "he who rejoices at [another's] disaster will not go unpunished."* Instead of waiting on God to elevate them at the appointed time, the bowed head of another Christian is a more desirable steppingstone to their next level. Overnight ministries and talk shows that are completely unordained by God are birthed all in a bid to use someone's shame as a steppingstone for success and popularity. God is not pleased. He will never inspire you to plot the downfall of someone else – even your enemy. What an exposure of our insecurities and identity crisis as Christians! Perfect public reputations covering crusty characters.

I know of families who have disowned their loved ones because they fell pregnant out of wedlock. Christian families by the way. Never mind what Jesus would do. They prize their reputation and standing within the community above the protection, love & covering of their daughter. It seems more desirable to cast her out than for them to be cast out of whatever social circles they currently find themselves in. God is not pleased. Thank God that His Word has this promise for us all: *"Although my father and my mother have forsaken me, yet the Lord will take me up [adopt me as His child]" (Psalm 27:10 AMP)*

I know of families who have forced their loved ones to secretly abort the baby without regard or thought of the lifelong repercussions of such an action. Christian families by the way. Never mind what Jesus would say. The quick fix cover up is more appealing to their senses and means life does not get complicated for them, or so they think and they can keep their beloved on the pre-planned track of school, career, marriage & children. In that order. Meanwhile their daughters never recover. They are scarred for life. God is not pleased. They don't seem to know or care that the Bible has this to say: *"And whoever causes one of these little ones (these believers) who acknowledge and cleave to Me to stumble and sin, it would be better (more profitable and wholesome) for him if a [huge] millstone were hung about his neck, and he were thrown into the sea" (Mark 9:42 AMP).*

I know of families who have forced their loved ones to get married at lighting speed when they discover the out of wedlock pregnancy in a bid to wrap up the shame they feel they have been caused in a more presentable packaging. Christian families by the way. Never mind what Jesus would think. It becomes about them and in all of this no one stops to think about the One who has always mattered the most from the beginning of time: Jesus. Instead, culture becomes God. A baby is not a reason to get married neither is the confusion that an unexpected child can bring, a good or strong foundation for any marriage. Instead of taking quality time to find out if the two want to get married then counselling and discipling them for a set season before pushing them down the altar - images are forcefully preserved. God is not pleased. Scripture is clear: *"If the foundations are destroyed, what can the [unyieldingly] righteous do, or what has He [the Righteous One] wrought or accomplished?" (Psalm 11:3 AMP).*

There is a time and place for culture but it must always be secondary to the Word of God. You and I have no right to condemn someone because at the end of the day we don't have a Heaven to give them neither are we the One who hung on a Cross for their sins. We have no right to name call, attack and abuse one another. We are not the judge neither are we the writer or re-writer of another person's destiny. You have your own salvation to work out & any excitement that you get from hearing that someone has fallen is a sign that something is greatly amiss in your own relationship with God. The saying goes: if you have nothing to say – PRAY. I say especially WHEN you have something to say: PRAY. You cannot genuinely spend time with God & still leave His presence with the desire to gossip. If you do, it wasn't Him that you encountered in the prayer room.

We must continually walk around with the consciousness that any sin committed by our fellow believer is an opportunity for us to be Christ like & extend His arms of love, bosom of peace & lips full of mercy as His body. It is our duty & we are all in need of mercy. God forbid we one day find ourselves in the very situation we mocked & celebrated when someone else was sinking in it. The Bible says: *"Then the King will say to those on His right hand, 'Come, you blessed of My Father, inherit the kingdom prepared for you from the foundation of the world: for I was hungry and you gave Me food; I was thirsty and you gave Me drink; I was a stranger and you took Me in; I was naked and you clothed Me; I was sick and you visited Me; I was in prison and you came to Me.' "Then the righteous will answer Him, saying, 'Lord, when did we see You hungry and feed You, or thirsty and give You drink? When did we see You a stranger and take You in, or naked and clothe You? Or when did we see You sick, or in prison, and come to You?' And the King will answer and say to them, 'Assuredly, I say to you, inasmuch as you did it to one of the least of these My brethren, you did it to Me'' (Matthew 25:34-40).*

Representing Christ is not majorly seen when we attend church on a Sunday morning in our Sunday best looking presentable before others. It is so easy to put on a perfected performance in church – too easy which is why church & God are not the same thing neither are they the same audience. Only one of those two see the inside of who you really are.

Representing Christ is seen in how we handle those who fall short of the standard of God. You are allowed to express disappointment if that is what you feel but there is a line that must not be crossed. With the Lord the sentence never ends at *"You knew better, what you have done is wrong and displeasing before my eyes."* No. He continually draws us with His lovingkindness and love can be found even in his anger. Love can be found in His disappointment. Love can be found in His pain. Therefore, it must be found in us and how we relate with those who have failed God.

Being a representative of Christ is seen in the hidden thoughts, opinions & judgements we harbour in our hearts each time we see and encounter people. It is seen in the secret conversations and discussions the walls of our house are privy to. In how we deal with the broken. How we comfort the grieving. How we stand with the afflicted. In what our response is when we receive a phone call that invites us to gossip about others. In what we share, screenshot & forward about other people to our friends DM & our group chats. It is seen. By God.

Perhaps you've had your sin spread like wildfire by people who professed to be Christians just like I did. Perhaps you began to be treated like an outcast by the very arms that should have covered you and helped you get yourself right with God.

Perhaps nobody ever asked how you were doing and how you were. Perhaps your trust in the church has been greatly shaken because of disappointment after disappointment. Perhaps you have been called all sorts of names under the Sun by the same lips that speak tongues on a Sunday morning. Perhaps you witnessed what your loved one went through at the hands of Christ's Bride & are determined to never allow that to happen to you. God can comfort your aches and pains and we are assured of this when Scripture tells us, *"He heals the brokenhearted and binds up their wounds" (Psalms 147:3).* Humans who fail to represent God well need the same mercy that you and I need so don't hold it against them. God is still good. Going to church is still right. God still loves you. God still has a plan for your life. God doesn't hold your past against you. God is waiting for you.

Please understand that we have an enemy. You do. I do. If he can succeed in isolating you from the places and the people that God designed to be a source of strength and encouragement to you then he is a step closer to wiping you out completely. The devil would rather have you turn your back on God and His people when you are mishandled and mistreated by people who should know better. However, the Bible says in Proverbs 11:14, *"Where there is no counsel, the people fall; but in the multitude of counsellors there is safety"* There is nothing more dangerous than going through a storm without at least one godly person to confide in and stand with you through it all. If I had not called my Aunty that day, I WOULD have committed abortion. Not maybe or perhaps. Definitely. I was weak and I needed someone emotionally, mentally & spiritually stronger than me. She was the voice of strength and reason I needed at the right time. You can't do life by yourself no matter how hurt you have been. We need each-other. I need you. You need me.

A vital principle to abide by is to always pray and ask God to connect you with people who can walk with you on your journey when you need extra support. The Bible says: *"The steps of a good man are ordered by the LORD, And He delights in his way" (Psalms 37:23).* If you speak to Him, He will speak to you. Be wise. Use that as an opportunity to cry out to God in prayer so that He sends you the RIGHT help. Understand that receiving the wrong help is a sign that there is right help out there and not a sign that there is no help altogether. Instead of throwing in the towel when you encounter bad people, ask God to connect you with the good. There ARE people who truly love God & His people. You will be surprised just how beautifully God can link you to the right people at the right time when it seems like all hope is lost. Try Him. He sees the pains and pressures you experience and He has people who are more than equipped to help walk you through it. Release the fear unto Him in prayer and call upon Him until help and support arrives. He will not disappoint you.

It can seem like such an impossibility to believe the loving words of a God you cannot see over the condemning words of Christians that you can see but, it is possible. God is not like man – He has not written you off or cancelled you from His list of people that He is madly in love with. He is not just a lover. He IS love. While they talk about you, God desires to talk to you. While they laugh at you, God desires to laugh with you. While they spread your story, God spreads His arms waiting for the moment you will run into them exactly the way that you are so He can fix you.

Change starts one person at a time and also one decision at a time. Decide that gossip dies when it gets to you. Decide to be the one that checks up on people when you hear of their sins.

Decide to intercede for them in the secret place and sow seeds that have eternal value. If Jesus had gone with the crowd on that fateful day in John 8 then the woman's story would have ended very differently. The crowd wanted her stoned to death. Jesus refused. It takes one person to stand up to the crowd. You can too.

The young lady lazily checked her phone to see who it was that was ringing. It had been a long excruciating day of sickness after sickness but she had managed to eat something. Though she knew that before bedtime it would be vomited out she rested in her temporary comfort. She was just about to watch something for the evening so who on earth wa-

'Mum'. She stared at her phone as it continued to ring. So, her Aunty had told them. She wasn't surprised. Obviously they had to know about her situation but that did nothing to still the heartbeat that was thundering beneath her chest or her now sweaty palms. What would she say? What could she say? She took the deepest breath of her life & answered the phone.

Some time later, long after the phone call had ended the girl still sat staring at her phone, tears streaming uncontrollably down her face. She couldn't quite articulate the emotions that she was feeling. It was all too overwhelming for her. So, she sat there, basking in the love of the Father. She still couldn't quite believe what she had heard with her own two ears.

"Aunty told us what has happened and is happening. Please don't kill that baby no matter who is pressuring you. You can get through this because God still has a plan for your life and He definitely has a plan for that baby. It doesn't matter what has happened – with God you can and will get through this. We are here. That's what family is for. Don't kill the baby. Don't do it."

She pressed replay in her mind over and over again as relief washed over her. She had held her breath at the start of the call as she braced herself for a conversation that was surely going to go as south as possible. But it seemed she had simply robbed herself unnecessarily of several seconds of wonderful fresh air. Where were the cultural lectures? The condemnation? The judgement? No 'how could you Shammah?' No name calling? No screaming or shouting?

She continued to bask. In a moment she became aware that this was how the Father felt about her as well. In fact, He felt it a million times more towards her than her parents ever could. He had no evil name to call her. He had no condemning label to stick on her forehead. He had nothing but love to extend.

So as the hours rolled by, the young lady forgot about her evening plans to watch whatever it is she had intended to watch. There was no other possible response to give after such a profound and life changing moment. Nothing else seemed to make sense and so later than evening as she laid in her bed, her face shiny with tears and one hand on her stomach – she finally broke the silence & spoke to Him.

I count myself most blessed to have parents who handled the news of my pregnancy with nothing but mercy, love and grace. To me they are Mum & Dad but to so many others they are Pastors. Yes, I am a Pastor's daughter. They could have placed their reputation above mine – they didn't. I imagined the worst possible reaction in the world – not because they are bad people but because of all of the mischief and escapades I had ever embarked on growing up – this latest one blew the roof off the building. It deserved a podium of it's own. A whole pregnancy Shammah. Wow.

I know for a fact that not many girls, especially of Zimbabwean origin or of African descent can ever dream of testifying of anything remotely similar. At some point they get labelled a prostitute, a whore and other unmentionable vile names that leave them internally scarred long after their child is born. Some get beaten up to a pulp and almost left for dead while others get kicked out to fend for themselves forever or are mercilessly dragged to the nearest clinic to have their unborn child ripped out from inside of them. Time moves on but their unhealed wounds don't and therefore keep them stuck at the sight of their rejection.

Their response reminded me of what I had forgotten: God loved me. There is nothing like having your arms up in self-defence, bracing yourself for a terrible collision only to be embraced instead with love. That is exactly how it felt when I spoke to my Mum that day. It is also how the woman caught in adultery would have certainly felt. From dread and mentally preparing herself to die to a clean slate the next second. All because of love. You are left speechless and in awe almost borderline confused because you are sure you are getting less than you deserve. Well, Jesus came and took what we deserved when He hung on the Cross so that we would get access to everything that we would otherwise have never deserved or qualified for in a million years by our own human efforts.

Imagine already battling with guilt, shame and condemnation within your own self then hearing those same thoughts brutally reinforced by those around you. Think about how that can destroy a person? Or do we bother to think at all? I can honestly say that being able to replay the words of encouragement from those who gave it to me is one of the major reasons I was able to come out of my pregnancy alive. I cannot imagine what would have become of me if I had nothing positive and godly to replay in my mind in those moments of silence and when I found myself facing sleepless night after sleepless night. The enemy made sure to be voice in my mind – something had to counter him.

You can begin a godly cycle by embracing those who have been rejected. You can begin a legacy of love. The seeds of love you sow in their life will one day be sown into another person's life, and another and another and so on all because you chose to go against the majority. The same way we are only able to love God because God first loved us (1 John 4:19), someone will one day be able to show a fellow believer love and mercy because you showed them love and mercy. The Bible says: *"Therefore I say to you, her sins, which are many, are forgiven, for she loved much. But to whom little is forgiven, the same loves little" (Luke 7:47).*

CHURCH let's be the church. For real. Your name calling will not change that what has happened has already happened. The screenshots, phone calls and videos you make will one day cease to be juicy, hot and relevant as time and life moves on. Meanwhile your brother /sister gets restored while you find yourself on the other side of the wrath of God over someone He forgave that you failed to show His love to though you bear the title CHRISTIAN. There is a proper way to process your disappointment and it's only in the presence of the Lord.

Condemnation has never led anyone to Christ. Ever. If there has ever appeared to be a change in someone after condemnation then it is only to falsely appease the condemning party and not because a true change has taken place. Think of your upbringing: the parent that was calm and communicated in love often saw better long-lasting results in their children than the one who screamed and name called out of anger. One was feared. One was loved. Think about it. It is not your job to convict a person – that is the job of the Holy Spirit. When we choose to adopt a "Neither Do We" stance to all who sin & fall short of the glory of God we partner with the Holy Spirit and leave room for Him to truly work on an individual's heart and mind.

We must stop desiring to be pleased first above the Lord because if a fallen person 'changes' for any reason aside from a deep-rooted desire to please the Lord – they haven't changed. Stop applying pressure so that YOU are pleased and satisfied with external results when the Holy Spirit wants to do a deep work in them from the inside out for HIS glory. Who are WE to be more disappointed in people than God is? Where are YOUR nail pierced hands?

We must understand that the end destination of those who fornicate without repenting is the same as the end destination of those who condemn the fornicators without repenting. No sin is bigger than another. We have ALL fallen short of God's glory and our approach must just change.

We are called to love. It is a commandment. 1 Corinthians 13:1-3 puts it beautifully when it says: *"Though I speak with the tongues of men and of angels, but have not love, I have become sounding brass or a clanging cymbal. And though I have the gift of prophecy, and understand all mysteries and all knowledge, and though I have all faith, so that I could remove mountains, but have not love, I am nothing. And though I bestow all my goods to feed the poor, and though I give my body to be burned, but have not love, it profits me nothing."*

A neither do we stance across the Body of Christ will bring about more change, revival and restoration in our families, communities and churches than we have ever seen with all of the condemnation we have been accustomed to dishing out. When we refuse to throw stones and respond with mercy and grace and a leading of souls back to Christ only then will husbands, wives, children, leaders and all begin to be truly transformed.

When we get out of the way, God can have His way!

----- CHAPTER FIVE -----

ACCOUNTABILITY

The young lady sat and listened respectfully to the advice they were both being given. In a short while they would officially share their breaking news with their Pastors.

"Just tell them you don't want this issue to be dealt with by them and that you want to handle it by yourselves in private."

The advice continued to pour in. Mostly unbiblical – but advice, nonetheless. The young lady knew of course the Pastors had to be the ones to take the reigns on the matter – that was who they were submitted to. Hiding their situation was not an option because of their level of responsibility within the Kingdom of God. However, respect was still due where it was due. Soon, the talk came to an end and they made their way to go and report themselves.

"Okay I understand." The Pastor began once the couple had finished speaking.

"Thank you for telling us. I will stand with you through this whole process, you can count on that & God will see us through."

The Pastor and his wife had listened intently as the couple had humbly narrated their situation and current status. No interruptions just patient patience.

"The rules of our church do however state that you have to go through church discipline. This means on a Sunday we decide and agree upon, between the 4 of us present in this room I will call both of your names and you will stand up from your seats and I will inform the congregation of what you have done and your situation. After this you will not be allowed to minister in church or accept any ministrations from other ministries for a certain period of time. During this time seek God earnestly concerning your situation. Now, the humility here is undeniable and I can see that God is already at work so while we would usually put you under discipline for a minimum period of 6 months plus, we have decided to only do so for 3 months. In those 3 months you are expected to meet with us regularly for prayer and counselling as well as keep us updated of all developments. Do we understand each other?"

The couple both nodded in agreement. The young lady felt relieved. She had hoped the conversation would go something like this as she had never agreed with people who continued to minister before the crowds without taking time to recover from their mess up first.

As the meeting concluded that day, the young lady noted how the talk of discipline had not made her feel condemned or afraid. With it had come a sense of peace. She supposed that it was the heart and motive behind the process. It was pure.

Two weeks later, on a windy Sunday morning, in front of the brethren: their discipline began.

I wholeheartedly believe that the process of church discipline we went through was for our own good. Many people would have (and have) left their church at the mention of having to stand up in a room full of people and have it announced that they were pregnant out of wedlock and submit to a process of restoration in that way however I was perfectly fine with it. A while earlier when I had confided in that other Pastor I had not been ready for people to know and neither had his motive been to play a part in my restoration journey. The spirit was all wrong. However, the heart of my new Pastors was. I felt at peace. If I didn't like the rules of the church when it came to discipline then I shouldn't have joined the church in the first place or better yet I should have lived right so discipline was something I would have never had to undergo.

I was and still am a leader in the Kingdom of God who had and does stand before God's people – so unless my plan was to run away to another country and change my identity (lol) it was going to eventually come to light that I was pregnant whether through channels of gossip, seeing my ever growing belly or a birthday post a few years down the line wishing my surprise daughter a happy birthday on the gram. I couldn't hide forever. An explanation had to be given. Luke 12:48 most definitely applied to me: *"…For everyone to whom much is given, from him much will be required; and to whom much has been committed, of him they will ask the more."* If I could stand before people and proclaim the Gospel then I could also stand before people and have it explained why I was no longer going to be standing before them and why I would be gaining obvious weight in the next few months to come.

A mature & transparent explanation by someone I was accountable to was also a form of protection for me believe it or not. Once an explanation was given publicly by our spiritual oversight -nobody came to us with a million questions because everything was out in the open. If they had, that would not only have been an assault on us but also a form of undermining the Pastor who had publicly spoken once and for all regarding our situation firstly in private to us and then in public for us. If one of the highest human authorities in our lives had spoken & made it known that he was aware as well as walking us through restoration and our issues in private then nobody else's contrary opinion had room to hold much weight.

You cannot be a successful Christian if you will not be accountable to anyone in authority over you. You are destined for certain deception and destruction if the only person that can tell you what to do is you. Yes, God speaks to us all on an individual basis but He designed this life in such a way that there is always someone sitting in a position of authority over you. Whether it is a parent over a child, a husband over a wife, a teacher over a student or an employer over an employee – society works better when we each do our part to abide by the principles of accountability, obedience and submission.

In the Bible we see many examples of accountability and submission and the benefits that resulted from it. Elisha was under Elijah. The 12 Disciples were under Jesus. Timothy was under Paul. The level of growth and maturity that became of each of the latter was as a direct result of following, listening, obeying & submitting to their respective former. We would be wise to follow the same example. Hebrews 13:17 says, *"Obey those who rule over you, and be submissive, for they watch out for your souls, as those who must give account. Let them do so with joy and not with grief, for that would be unprofitable for you."* We avoid danger by listening to those who have walked the road before us and gain an advantage. Only a fool insists on making their own mistakes. Save yourself time.

Now I have to be honest I did not get the whole submission thing correct 100% during this entire journey. One night as I reached breaking point within myself because of some of the things that were being done to me and my unborn baby, I texted one of my girlfriends and within 2 hours I had packed a large suitcase and left to go to her house. Pregnant hormonal Shammah was convinced it was for good as she wobbled down the stairs and out of the house in the middle of the night. However, I returned after several emotional weeks. I left for another city without saying a single word to my Pastors though and this was highlighted to me. It's either I was going to be completely submissive or I was not.

You must be someone who can be corrected, guided and taught if you are ever to become the person God created you to be. You don't know everything there is to know about God. Neither do I. Nor any Pastor on this Earth. We know in part. Hence the reason we all need each other in one way or the other. An inability to receive correction and guidance from those older, wiser or mature than you in the things of God will lead you to end up in the same boat as those individuals I mentioned earlier who were never taught about or allowed to face proper consequences while growing up.

Another thing to note is that public discipline goes hand in hand with seeking God in secret behind closed doors. Just because we were made to stand up in front of the congregation one Sunday morning didn't mean that we were sorry or had repented. It did not mean that our hearts had been changed either. It was simply part of the process (an important part) and a prompt so to speak in the right direction but the greater work was what we were doing behind closed doors. Matthew 15:8 says: *"These people draw near to Me with their mouth, And honour Me with their lips, But their heart is far from Me."* There would have been absolutely no point in ticking the box of standing up on that Sunday and the 3 months that followed just to appease man while God was displeased with the posture of my heart and my life in secret. The public only mattered if it was backed with God's presence in private.

I had failed to repent properly by turning to God properly some months before and this was yet another prompt for me to do so. Repentance is always an inward work before it is an outside work however because of our stubbornness sometimes it takes outside events to prompt us to change on the inside. I think that we can all agree that there is a level of pain & vulnerability that drives you into the arms of God in a way that nothing else can. Sadly, sometimes that's what it takes because as humans we can be so set in our sinful ways no matter how patient and merciful God is. I strongly believe that the process of discipline aided in my seeking of the Lord during what was a very difficult time.

There were no longer any ministry engagements to hide behind. There were no more skilfully and colourfully designed flyers with glamorous pictures of me to parade on social media. My friendship circle drastically reduced almost overnight. I mean, people quickly deleted pictures with wonderful captions they had posted about me. It was safer to quickly disassociate with me. Every single invitation to minister was declined. Every last one. TV hardly interested me; I could barely focus. Everything that had stopped me from presenting myself before the feet of Jesus and allowing Him to fix me was now gone. It was simply me, my sin & my Saviour.

It was not disappointing to hear that we had to refrain from public ministry for a set season. Pride could have assisted me in digging up some sort of indignation at the very thought of even having to be stood up for all the church to see but the truth is I was tired. I needed to stop. I was extremely tired. And I needed to be as far away as possible from a microphone and as near to the Cross as possible. My soul needed refreshing and reviving in a way that only time spent with Jesus could do. I had no pour left within me. I was relieved at the chance to be forced to take a break otherwise I fear I may have just carried on and on like that kite I mentioned earlier. And while a public announcement did not necessarily mean that I was repentant, it was a shove in the right direction and an opportunity for me to use the stillness and silence for the right reason which was to seek Gd. So even though the 3 months came and passed, it was 11 months before I accepted an invitation and 15 months before I stepped out anywhere to preach. I needed time with God.

The church I was attending during that season is one of the few that I know to have some sort of disciplinary and accountability system in place. Many don't. It seems to be that if we are not throwing stones of condemnation to fellow believers for their sins and writing them off for good then we are on the complete opposite end of the scale and turning a very blind eye to the error of their ways and allowing things that need to be addressed to go unaddressed without anyone being held responsible. I cannot tell you how many tales I know of affairs, rape, molestation, bullying, fraud that have gone completely ignored as though nothing happened. Yes. In the church. There is an extreme lack of balance.

Proverbs 27:23 reminds all shepherds to *"know well the condition of your flocks and pay attention to your herds."* We were fortunate enough to have our Pastors living a comfortable distance away for the both of us. We were in their house sometimes several times a week for prayer, counselling, discussions etc… to ensure that the 3 months of discipline were not wasted or just for show.

The Bible says in Galatians 6:1-2, *"Brethren, if a man is overtaken in any trespass, you who are spiritual restore such a one in a spirit of gentleness, considering yourself lest you also be tempted. Bear one another's burdens, and so fulfil the law of Christ."* The word RESTORE that you see used in this verse is the Greek word "kartarizo" and it means to: *strengthen, equip or make one what he ought to be.* That is what we are called to do as the Body of Christ when a fellow believer falls. To restore them with the Word of God, fellowship, praying for them and with them, sound teaching and encouragement until they are strong in their faith, equipped to fight the good fight of Faith once again as well as become who they are supposed to be in Christ.

Restoring someone is not overlooking their wrong deeds, making light of them or pushing everything under the carpet in the name of love. Love is quite the opposite actually. Love is honest. Love confronts. Love addresses. In fact, it is not even possible to properly restore someone without confronting their sin first, the roots of it and dealing with the situation from the inside out or the bottom up. It is not about exposure – it is about reconciling a stray sheep back to the Good Shepherd: Jesus (John 10:14). It is everything to do with meeting a person where they have fallen & helping them to rise again step by step through the guidance of the Holy Spirit.

Perhaps your church does things differently? Maybe they don't stand you up in front of everyone but definitely excuse you from any sort of service or position that involves you leading or ministering to people? Don't harden your heart.

I remember something I witnessed in church when I was about 11 or so years old. One Sunday, the Pastor read aloud a letter on behalf of a young lady to the entire congregation. I didn't understand much of it to be honest – I was young, but I remember discerning a very sombre and serious atmosphere in the room as the letter was read. Now I know it was a letter of explanation and apology from the youth leader because she was pregnant out of wedlock. That was a part of the particular process of the church she was submitted to. Whatever the process is wherever you find yourself, submitting to it will be for your own good. I would be concerned if there was nothing in place to help restore you after you have sinned. Nothing to hold you accountable for your actions. Nothing to aid you in seeking God on a deeper level when you've seriously missed the mark. Just life as usual as though nothing ever happened. Such churches you should run away from because they do not have the condition of your soul as number one priority. Where your gift is celebrated without your character being confronted – FLEE.

People will talk. They definitely will and guess what? They still do. Choosing to do things the right way "from now onwards" after you have sinned will not stop people from talking about you or throwing mud at your name. It's not about people though it is about staying focused on pleasing God. The One who sees and rewards in due course.

Galatians 6:9 is a beautiful promise we can hold onto no matter where we find ourselves: *"And let us not grow weary while doing good, for in due season we shall reap if we do not lose heart."* Take your mind off of what you can get out of the whole process and focus more on what you can give to God through it all. He wants your heart. A break from preaching means nothing if He doesn't have your heart. A deactivated social media account means nothing if He doesn't have the entirety of your affections. Anything done on the outside for God means absolutely nothing to Him if it is not an honest reflection of what is taking place on the inside for Him.

One of the most popular statements of defence used when people don't want to abide by any process of discipline and ultimately restoration is the following: *"At the end of the day, my sin is between me and God. It is nobody else's business!"* Wrong. As much as I made sure to stress earlier on on this book that your priority after sinning is God and should always be God – that does not mean that people don't matter at all. They do. Just, AFTER God. The whole aim of Christianity is to win souls to the Kingdom of God. People matter. Ultimately your relationship with God will always overflow and affect the people around you whether for good or for bad. Therefore, when we fail, we must own up, make amends when we can and be humble. The following Scriptures show us the importance of living aware (not bound or imprisoned) that people are watching us and many looking to us for guidance in their own walks with God:

"You are the salt of the earth; but if the salt loses its flavour, how shall it be seasoned? It is then good for nothing but to be thrown out and trampled underfoot by men" (Matthew 5:13).

"Let your light so shine before men, that they may see your good works and glorify your Father in heaven" (Matthew 5:16).

"Likewise, exhort the young men to be sober-minded, in all things showing yourself to be a pattern of good works; in doctrine showing

integrity, reverence, incorruptibility, sound speech that cannot be condemned, that one who is an opponent may be ashamed, having nothing evil to say of you" (Titus 2:6-8).

"Having your conduct honourable among the Gentiles, that when they speak against you as evildoers, they may, by your good works which they observe, glorify God in the day of visitation." (1 Peter 2:12).

Zacchaeus had an encounter with Jesus in Luke 19 which led him to not only follow Jesus with his whole heart but to also address the people he had stolen from and make rightful amends by repaying them back 4 times as much. It is not possible to encounter the true God and not be compelled to live with a sober awareness of the people around us and how our actions affect them. It may not aways be practical or in your power to make amends but it is always in your power to be humble and to apologise. We don't get to pick and choose the parts that we prefer.

Interestingly, the same people who have the biggest issue with some of the protocols of order within the church will happily submit to their bosses at work, submit to a boyfriend who is not their husband nor has any intention of becoming their husband and submit to the ungodly expectations of society in terms of their dressing, language and choice of friends. Only the things of God seem to arouse what we feel is a righteous anger but in reality is the spirit of rebellion. There is the false notion that the house of God is the one place we should be able to do what we want, how we want & in the way we want to do it under the guise of "love." No. *"But all things must be done appropriately and in an orderly manner" (1 Corinthians 14:40).* Order begins in the house of God!

----- CHAPTER SIX -----

STONE HER!

The young lady was so deeply focused on watching her TV programme that at first she didn't even notice the telephone conversation that was taking place in the room solely for her benefit, a few metres away from her. Many months later, heart still broken she wished she had not heard it.

"You know, the young people of this generation. They will be out here taking glamorous pictures meanwhile their lives are something else. Well, I don't like dirty people. I can tell a dirty person from a mile away & I am not deceived. I don't fall for such nonsense. They laze about... I don't tolerate such rubbish. And the way that they smell - proper stinking. Absolute filth..."

The voice went on and on in their native language like a pandora's box that had been opened. It unleashed all its disapproval, disgust & dislike for the young lady who sat nearby – no longer watching TV but doing her best to fight back the tears that threatened to escape from her tired eyes. She wrestled hard to maintain her composure. There was no way she was going to show him that his words had cut to the very core of her being. There was no way she was going to show that the babe inside her was responding to her distress and beginning to kick hard against her belly. Almost as if to say: "say something mum! Defend yourself! He has no right! Speak up mummy. Mummy!"

She consoled herself by telling herself over and over again that her name had not been directly mentioned so his words could have been about anybody on this Earth. But she knew he was referring directly to her. Everybody knew. The private apologies and excuses made on his behalf that came later confirmed they all knew. She patiently waited for the phone call to end then forced herself to linger for an unsuspicious while longer so her exit could not be connected to his phone call. Quietly and brokenly the young lady retreated upstairs to release her anguish into a pillow. When was this going to end?

The other day it had been a large, empty water bottle thrown in her direction as she stood making something to eat, because she had forgotten to take it out with the recycling. It missed her by a few inches. Another occasion she had been denied food that was within arm's length after being on her feet almost all day working hard and so she had to wait an extra hour plus close to midnight to get a takeaway instead of the home cooked meal. She was pregnant for goodness sake!

If it wasn't her polite 'Good Morning' being blatantly ignored then it was the overly critical analysis of anything she put her hands to do. Her attitude changed. She was not gonna bother. If they were gonna talk it was better they had something true to actually talk about. Emptying the heavy bin was beginning to take a toll on her back as her pregnancy progressed and yet arms with more than enough strength for her and the unborn babe she carried would watch in judgement as she struggled to make her way towards the bins.

Another evening it had been an iPad flung at her and her unborn babe. She had to call the ambulance. Another, she shielded her belly from rage filled kicks. She had to call the ambulance. The third, her calves and arms had received the hottest slaps and left her bruised for days. She had called the ambulance. She fell down the stairs one day. The response…

"Why did you use the house phone to make a call after falling down the stairs. You should not have done that. Look at the price of my bill now."

Her attitude hardened and little by little the pain began to filter out through her words. A clapback, a sigh or an eyeroll for every inch of mistreatment. The least she could do was try to defend herself. She owed that to her unborn child. She couldn't afford to be weak. She was tired. When was this going to end?

"What do you do to deserve beatings while pregnant?"

"It's just bringing shame to yourself when you speak and tell of the beatings and what happens behind closed doors. People will laugh. Keep it to yourself. It's embarrassing."

Her heart went ice cold. It was becoming too much for her to bear. Each day was a struggle and any excuse to stay buried away in her bedroom she would use. Sickness? Sure, why not. Fatigue? Why not? 'I didn't sleep the whole night so I am going to spend today catching up on sleep in my room?' Why not? Anything to ease the strain. Anything to avoid the way her heartbeat with fear and dread most mornings when it was time to emerge from her bedroom or each time she heard a car pull into the driveway. She never knew what each day had in store. Maybe she was better off not being on this Earth anymore. Maybe, just maybe…

It was one thing to be aware that other people were slowly coming into the know about my pregnancy and were most definitely talking about me in disapproval from many miles away in their various houses and countries and another thing altogether to go through daily verbal attacks, abuse & rejection in my face because I was pregnant. It is a lot easier when you can control and limit your exposure to those who don't like you by retreating to the safety and privacy of your own house – but how about when there is nowhere to retreat for one reason or the other?

From that beautiful day when I had the phone call with my Mum when I was able to enter into the Lord's presence I went back to square one. I allowed the storm around me to snatch me back out of God's presence and so what should have been a relocation into Abba's arms turned into a temporary visit. Again. I know I am not the only one to go through this. There have been many before me and there will continue to be many after me. It is hard to regain your strength when it is constantly being attacked every single day. It is almost impossible to reach a place of stability when your world continues to be tossed violently without warning. It is terrifying to walk on eggshells daily as you grow another human being inside you. And this was my experience for a vast portion of my pregnancy.

I cannot tell you how many tears I cried. All I can say is that I would cry until my body ached then I would worry endlessly about my unborn child and how much I was affecting her on the inside of me and the guilt would pile on all the more. The enemy had turned things up a notch in the arrows he was throwing my way. All of the relief I felt on the day I spoke to my Mum vanished as a godly moment was successfully overshadowed by a daily living hell.

See, guilt is mostly a focus on what you have done but shame is everything to do with who the devil begins to tell you that you are because of what you have done. Shame is a gross attack on your identity as feelings of worthlessness come in and a strong conviction that you are indeed dirty, a failure & unforgiveable settle over you. I was desperate for relief. I was desperate to hear words of life. I was desperate to be consistently reminded that God valued me & loved me & forgave me. From anyone.

So where is Jesus when we are facing daily, continuous suffering? I had opened the door to this but did that mean I would suffer indefinitely? Where is He when we have no break or relief from our tormentors and the lies they have to tell? Is He there as the wind and waves gather momentum and threaten to utterly devour us? No really… is He? It's one thing to be able to quote Romans 8:28 and say: *"all things work together for good to those who love God, to those who are the called according to His purpose"* long after things have worked together. It's another thing altogether to mean it and feel it with every fibre of your being IN the storm when everything looks hopeless. Let me tell you, I didn't feel a single letter of that entire verse. All I felt was pain and rejection that seemed to have no expiry date. I wanted to die. So again, I ask, where is Jesus? Where was He?

In Mark 4:31-41 we read about the time when Jesus and His disciples were in a boat trying to cross from one side of the shore to the other. A heavy storm began and in their understandable panic and distress the disciples turned to see Jesus – the One with all of the answers – fast asleep like a baby. Imagine that? He was asleep as what appeared to be certain destruction confronted them. Asleep & silent. They woke Him up – as any on us would do, and though He did calm the wind and the waves for them, guess what His final statement to them concerning the whole situation was: *"Why are you so fearful? How is it that you have no faith?"*

It surprised Jesus that they still had not reached an understanding that no evil could ever overpower them in His presence. His silence did not equate to His absence. They simply had to trust Him. By now they should have known who He was and what He was capable of doing. However, they allowed the display of power by the storm to lead them to forget that the origin of ALL power was right there in their boat. Think about it! What were the chances that the boat was going to result in all of their deaths when Jesus was in the boat with them? Silent but present. He was there all along but the storm blinded them to the reality of His presence. They could not and would not believe that His presence was enough. They forgot that after all, He was the One who created the creation that was acting up so how could creation ever overpower the Creator? They forgot.

I must admit, I forgot too. I forgot that the loudest in a room isn't necessarily the strongest. The silence of Christ's presence in that boat was always going to be more powerful than the volume of the storm. I allowed the continuous harsh words and disgusting treatment to settle deep within my soul and grow along with my belly and a very heavy bitterness and resentment to begin to grow on the inside of me. I forgot that God was the One who had perfectly fashioned and formed my heart and so was able to bring it back to a calm, resting pace as the fear of leaving my bedroom overtook me every single morning – if I gave it to Him.

I forgot that there was nothing wrong with retreating back to my bedroom to cry as often as I did but it was better to cry out to Jesus in the safety of His presence so it counted for something.

So, my ashes stood a fighting chance of being turned into beauty. I forgot that I didn't have to be intimidated by the presence of any man because angels were at my beck and call. I forgot that I had a greater Name to call upon for every name I was called. I forgot there were beautiful nail pierced hands to soothe my own skin after it reddened from the latest slap, punch or push. I forgot that the night I packed my bags to leave and go away to a girlfriend's house who immediately dropped everything in the dead of night & drove to collect me as I expressed my fears to her, Jesus was longing to have me run into His loving arms and actually TRY Him. I forgot that the terrifying night when 2 grown men came head to head, voices raised – one with blood boiling, fists clenched and more than ready to violently fight the other in me and my unborn baby's honour – the God of angel armies wanted me to allow Him to take over & come to my lasting rescue. The rescuing of everything internal. I forgot that those 3 powerful words from Jesus overrode anyone who still dared desire to throw stones at me. He was always there with me. Day in. Day out. Always. But, I simply wanted it all to end – immediately without delay.

I sunk into a very low place as the days rolled by and a newfound compassion for those who have ever committed suicide or come close to it was birthed in my heart. Suicide is a notion that slowly and quietly enters the mind of s/he that is fully convinced that there is no more hope. It stays there for weeks or months, growing and growing slowly as your situation worsens until it begins to feel like common sense. Thoughts of hopelessness, self-pity, shame, fear and desperation add fuel to the fire. The enemy begins to make suggestions: pills, train tracks, bleach, poison and so forth.... For the oppressed heart and mind it becomes a twisted form of comfort to know that a way out is in their control at the click of a finger because everything else in their life does not seem to be. Day in and day out until one gives in…

But God is faithful. He is the kind of God who comes to the rescue and the aid of His children. The kind of God who can go to the extent of giving someone you have not even spoken to or shared your burden with, a crystal clear dream exposing the raging warfare that is taking place in your mind. Someone who God uses to speak truth and life into you until every last bit of darkness is expelled. One who is used to bring to pass the Scripture that says, *"And the light shines in the darkness, and the darkness did not comprehend it" (John 1:5).* Suddenly a seemingly certain appointment with death is cancelled and one goes onto live and declare the works of the Lord.

I am reminded of the story of Hagar in Genesis 16 (read the whole chapter). She faced daily, cruel mistreatment from her boss, Sarai during her pregnancy until it all became too much for her to bare and so she decided to run away. However, an angel from the Lord then appeared to her after she thought she had done the right thing by going as far away as possible with two things for her. The first was an instruction from God to go back to her boss. The same boss who had been mistreating her. The second was a promise from God about the child she was carrying. I know for a fact that I would have argued back and presented my case along with the many receipts of why I should not go back. But, Hagar obeyed and returned.

We are not told if Sarai's attitude towards her changed. Maybe it did, maybe it didn't but what we are definitely told is that she had a Word and a promise from God. What is interesting to note is that Hagar was partly responsible for the treatment that Sarai was giving her. The Bible tells us that

"...when she saw that she had conceived, her mistress became despised in her eyes" (Genesis 16:4). Hagar started the entire fight – she was the guilty party but when things backfired she couldn't handle it anymore. She was as guilty as me and my pregnant self were but in His mercy, God found her and He spoke.

Could it be that no matter how dark the situation is – if you have God, He is more than enough? If you can allow His conviction to reach you then He will be more than enough for whatever the rest of your journey will look like? Could it be that if God is requiring you to be uncomfortable for a season it is because He is going to sustain you through it even if you were wrong? Remember He is a good Father so He would not have set her up to perish on the other end of obeying His instruction.

There is nothing to be valued more than receiving a Word from God in the midst of a situation that looks like it is going to be the end of you. The Word will give you strength and courage when you are sure you cannot go another day in that situation. A Word from God assures you that you are secure in Him no matter what is being thrown your way. A Word of God gives you something to fight the enemy off with when he comes whispering in your ear that you are utterly finished. It enables you to remain standing even when it defies human logic. It gives you something to whisper over and over to yourself when it seems like the midnight hour is never going to pass.

Let's say we know for certain that Sarai continued to mistreat Hagar and cause her great pain. I picture a newfound level of resilience in Hagar compared to the first time around before she had ran away. Why? Because she had a Word. A Word she could whisper to herself late at night to comfort herself in her bed if that particular day had been tougher than usual. A Word she could recite over and over to strengthen herself in the middle of the Summer heat as she worked tirelessly probably to the demands of a boss which were designed to break her. A Word she could sing to herself in many different melodies to encourage herself when the bad treatment threatened to blur out the picture of the future God had promised her. A word. Something that could never be taken away from her.

Do not mistaken my words. I am not saying you must stay in situations that you deem to be abusive or dangerous. By all means, if you can get to a safe place – DO SO. However, maybe you are in a situation where you have no other option but to stay? At work? At school? At home? At church? Not necessarily a dangerous one but an uncomfortable one perhaps? A stressful one? A difficult one? A challenging one? God is aware of all of the above and more. Is it so crazy to believe that He is able to carry you through? Is it such a wild thought to truly believe with all of your heart that His hand can reach you even in your seemingly impossible situation? Some have the luxury of being able to run away and stay away – others have the honour of choosing to trust God through it all and seeing His magnificent power displayed.

This is why I keep emphasising spending time in the presence of God and waiting on Him. He will only speak to those who lean their ears on His chest to hear His heartbeat and discern His will in that particular moment. Confusion does not have to win over you. Hagar's friends may have all advised her "*Girl leave! You deserve better! Your boss is so out of order!*" All factually correct mind you but it still turned out that God had something else in mind for her life. Hear from God before running with the opinions and advice of man – you may just be surprised to hear what He has to say to you about your specific situation.

As my treatment worsened, the primary battlefield was not my womb – it was my mind. If I could be defeated up there, I was already defeated anywhere else. The devil knew this. My thoughts were plagued and troubled and confused and no amount of motivational talk could dig me out of the ditch I seemed to be sinking deeper into as the days passed by. The Shammah that had encouraged so many others in similar situations previously was nowhere to be found. I became a shadow of a shell of the girl I once was. I couldn't fathom that Jeremiah 29:11 which says: *"For I know the thoughts that I think toward you, says the LORD, thoughts of peace and not of evil, to give you a future and a hope."* – still stood over my life. How could it? Thoughts that my actions had surely killed any chance of me ever becoming plagued me daily…

What I did not immediately come to realise was that The Lord wanted me to lean into Him and discover a side of Him I had never encountered in my life before. It didn't matter how far and wide I had travelled in His name – there was always going to be more about God to discover & encounter. All along, I had been very good at speedily removing myself from situations and people that I deemed uncomfortable and painful, similar to Hagar. Anything I was not impressed with & I was gone. I made sure to 'protect my space' to the point that I also kept God and His desired dealings with me out.

I had mostly only ever experienced the safety, comfort and strength He has to give AFTER whatever storm it was, was over but never IN the middle of the storm. I knew how to go to Him for healing and mending when the pain of the situation finally caught up with me long after – but at the time of the offence, betrayal & hurt I would rarely take His hand. I would handle things my way first and see how that went then remember

Him. If it was too painful to confront and deal with then I would put it on the shelf and see to it another time. There was no running away this time though. I had to trust Him.

The same way Peter began to sink into the sea the moment he took his eyes off Jesus' in Matthew 14:30 is how I sunk daily the more I kept my eyes focused on the horrible treatment I was receiving. Listen, it was bad. Some things can not be put on paper. Until I began to put my eyes continually on Him, life was up and down for a long time. I would get a special reminder of God's love for me today but by tomorrow find myself back to that low and depressed place a few days later. No stability. Still refusing to completely turn TO Him. All I could see were my surroundings and not Jesus right in the middle of all that had gone wrong and was still going wrong. My incorrect point of focus meant that I felt alone and abandoned by a God who was there all along but simply waiting for me to shift my gaze upwards. It wasn't supposed to be about what I could see all around me – but WHO I should have chosen to look at.

I cannot imagine how Peace felt as He looked at the raging storm in my life that He was more than equipped to handle. I don't know how Mercy felt as He watched me carry my backpack of sin & guilt day in and day out. I'll never know how Love felt as He watched the Him-shaped-hole deep in my heart that He came to fill get bigger and bigger with each passing day. He was there. Ever faithful as always.

When you read the story of the woman caught in adultery in John 8 you'll find that while her accusers thought they had humiliated her by bringing her before Jesus in front of the crowd they didn't realise that they in fact positioned her to receive the very thing that she needed: His mercy and forgiveness. While they thought that her head would be forever bowed low in shame, they didn't realise that her brokenness and posture attracted Jesus to her. Unbeknown to them they brought her before the judge (Psalm 7:11) & the defence lawyer (Jeremiah 50:34) all rolled into one. Imagine that. The perfect date with destiny. There is a level of lowness where the only way is up especially when you are a child of God. They forgot that God is *"near to those who have a broken heart and saves such as have contrite spirit" (Psalm 34:18).* Her humble state was the highway He needed to ride on in and change absolutely everything about her. While they thought they had won one over her, they were blinded to the victory they had positioned her for.

God's presence IS enough for every situation that we go through. *"You will show me the path of life; In Your presence is fullness of joy; At Your right hand are pleasures forevermore" (Psalms 16:11).* His presence is enough for every tear you have ever had to shed with no one to comfort you. It is enough for the deep cuts in your heart that seem like they will never heal. He is enough for the words you think you will never forget for as long as you live. His presence is enough for the names that you have been called. It is enough for the places, people and circles that you have been rejected from. It is enough for the chapters of your life that you have had to navigate without protection and covering. His presence is enough for the confusion and heaviness that does not seem to have an expiry date in your life. It is enough for the strength you need to honour Him amid that difficult situation.

His presence is enough for you to receive inner peace so you can begin to walk with your head held high again as though nothing ever happened. His presence is enough for the guilt you carry without a chance to ever put it down. It is enough for the shame you bear that means you walk around with a certain defensiveness to your character and attitude. His presence is enough for the condemnation that pretends like it has gone away only for it to surface within you at the most unexpected times. His presence is enough. It is more than enough and if you will trust Him, draw near to Him – you will feel Him closer than a mother feels her breastfeeding babe. You will feel Him because He is more than enough and He has always been more than enough for both you and me, no matter what we have done or how far we've gone.

Nevertheless, my struggle continued. Some days I would feel tough enough to bear the blows – other times I just couldn't bare it. One precious day – a day I will never forget, when I was failing to take what was coming my way I was in the kitchen washing the dishes and with tears streaming down my face I asked God a serious question from inside of my heart: *"Lord, am I still your princess?"* It sounds like a strange question to most of you reading this but between me and God it made perfect sense. Think of it as 2 lovers with their own secret code & language for each other. In the same way a husband will refer to their wife as "buttons" or "candy floss" and it makes no sense to the rest of the universe but just know that there is a story there. History. I continued washing up, following my mind as it roamed from thought to thought. After a while, to avoid being alone with my thoughts which were landing on nothing but more guilt and shame, I tuned in to a Facebook live stream by an Apostle I knew and busied my self some more in the kitchen. His voice and the accompanying worship music were the perfect sound to invade my sad thoughts. Then out of nowhere I heard:

"Shammah. Shammah. Shammah." I almost dropped the cutlery I was holding. The sound was coming from my phone. It was the Apostle:

"I hear the Lord telling me to tell you that you are His princess. Yes, you are His princess. He calls you His princess."

Sounds like something out of a movie right? I kid you not – that is exactly what He said to me on Facebook Live. I actually couldn't believe what I was hearing. My heart pounded away in my chest and my hand stood over my mouth in shock. Had I really just silently asked the Lord a question and was now receiving an audible response through this man of God minutes later? My heart continued to beat as I listened to everything else God had to say to me through his servant. He spoke for a little while longer about many different things but the 5 words that I will never forget are:

"YOU ARE STLL MY PRINCESS"

Wow. A Word from God. My Word from God. I began to weep in worship there and then in that kitchen. Again, God had reached for me. I was gobsmacked. Abba had reached out for me. Abba. There was hope. He wanted His lover back. The one who used to know without a shadow of a doubt that His presence was more than enough for her every need. He wanted her back. His song over me was still one of love and mercy. He loved me. Deeply. I was loved!

Sometimes we are waiting for some more seemingly bigger revelation or breaking news. But I promise you there is nothing more precious to be realised nor a more powerful truth to be grasped than the fact that God loves you. When it hits your heart in a fresh way that you are beautifully loved as imperfect as you are – your world changes. Though you should have known better. Though you deliberately disobeyed. You. Are. Loved.

I am reminded of the prodigal son in Luke 15:11-32 and just how he must have felt to know that after all he had done and just how far he had strayed, his father was still madly in love with him. True love is a difficult thing to put into words. How does one begin to repay such a love? The kind that you don't qualify for in any way, shape or form? In verse 21 when he was sure that he was no longer fit to be called his fathers son, his father was simply filled with pure joy that he had come home. Logic would have said, make the son earn his way back into the family. Logic would have said make the son earn his fathers love and heart again. Logic would have disowned him for life or at least a season in order to teach him a great and unforgettable lesson. Logic would have displayed just a little show of spite to express the extent of the pain he caused. Love had other ideas. Love welcomed him back home with open arms. Love publicly celebrated his return in glorious fashion. Love, still called him son with beaming pride.

Here is when I changed. Yes, me. My situation was not going to change. I was pregnant – that wasn't changing any time soon until my day of delivery. Whoever disliked me was probably not going to miraculously wake up adoring me. I could however take Jesus' hand & allow Him to walk me through. I could allow Him to change my perspective. I could allow Him to be the fourth man in the fire I was currently standing in. He wasn't interested in sharing my burden with me. He wanted to take it from me. All of it: *"casting all your care upon Him, for He cares for you" (1 Peter 5:7).*

I prayed asking God to forgive me for distancing myself from Him. I asked for forgiveness for neglecting His Word. I said sorry for ignoring Him each time He had whispered for me to come. I asked Him to forgive me for not praying. I told Him how much I missed Him. I finally admitted that the weight of my sin was too much for me to carry & I was ready to make the exchange for life. I told Him I was ready to take my eyes and ears off of what people were saying and would forever say and fix them onto Him. We talked about the deep pain I felt. I shared my fears, the ones I could never dream of sharing with a human being. As simply as a child I opened up, hiding nothing from my Abba. We worked through the warnings He had given me but I ignored, I said sorry. We talked about the internal and external wounds I had acquired along the way as my bump grew bigger and bigger. We addressed the real reasons why I ended up pregnant. We addressed the state of my heart long before I got pregnant. We addressed it all. I gave it all over to Him. I told Him about the guilt that wouldn't lift off me. I gave Him the shame. I gave Him everything.

He told me that I was forgiven. He told me to forget about what HE was now calling the past. He told me my future was secure in Him. He told me that He would never leave me nor forsake me. He told me that He loved me. He told me that He would bring me out with a testimony of His mercy & grace. He told me I would recover all. He gave me so many promises I wrote them down in a book I still have today and then He reminded me to go back to what He had said to me before I got pregnant and assured me that it all still stood and that He would fulfil every last word.

I spoke to Him. He spoke to me. Day in and day out. It literally looked as simple as starting my day with Him with my Bible and notebook open and talking to Him. It looked like no longer silently cussing back at my abusers in my heart but turning them into prayer points instead. It looked like becoming as simple as a child before Him and forgetting everything that I thought I knew and allowing Him to teach me afresh. It looked like dragging myself to his feet on the days the enemy's voice seemed to be on loudspeaker and fighting it out there. It looked like what many would call going back to the basics of Christianity when in actual fact those are the fundamentals and the things we should never graduate from doing. Things which many lose and neglect in their search for the 'deep things' and the 'big things' of God not knowing that He is the big thing. The only thing. I fell back in love with Jesus, His presence, opening my Bible and not only reading it but living it & praying aloud with my own mouth.

And little by little the darkness that had been hanging over me began to leave. My mind cleared as the thoughts that troubled me silently, lost their power. And one by one the volume of those desperately wanting to throw stones was silenced – not because they stopped speaking but because I began to hear what Abba had always been saying. Not because they no longer desired to do so but simply because my eyes were now firmly fixed on Jesus. And anyone who has ever locked eyes with Him knows that absolutely everything else ceases to matter. It was in the silence of my then bedroom with my growing bump that me, my sin and their stones came face to face with the Saviour – it was the perfect date with destiny.

Please hear me… human beings only made the smaller percentage of those desiring to stone me. There were and are bigger enemy's than the girl who makes an indirect status about you or the Pastor who airs your business out for the whole world to know and so on. Depression wanted its fair shot at me too. Backsliding never to return was waiting in queue for the go ahead to hit me. Failure, anxiety, fear, rejection, sickness, an unfulfilled destiny, a still birth… they all waited & waited. But God.

From then on two lovers were reunited and a soul once darkened with shame began to sing again. Some days I would sprint to His presence and other days I would pep talk myself through every last one of the pregnancy symptoms and fatigue with a resolute *"girl, you better get where you need to get to."* It didn't matter which of the two it was on any given day, the point is I would reach Him. I was no longer afraid and I was no longer hiding from the Omnipresent God.

----- CHAPTER SEVEN -----

TIIANA – A GIFT FROM GOD

The young lady stared at the screen in complete disbelief. She still could not believe that she was looking at her child. As the sonographer continued to perform the ultrasound scan she could just about keep herself from wobbling with glee. That was her baby. Her princess. Her heritage from the Lord. She could not contain her joy and excitement – it was like something out of this world. She was about to become somebody's whole mother!

"Oh my gosh, look. Our baby. I can't believe it!" The young lady carried the excitement of the scan with her long after it was over. Weeks and months. It made the days seem short as her labour drew near. It made the animosity seem less significant. She was thrilled. The silver lining in the midst of all of the chaos & confusion that was taking place around her. Her baby. Her child.

One mildly sunny day on her way to buy her regular craving of a tuna baguette and some fresh orange juice from the local bakery, she spoke to God.

"Lord, I know you have a name for this child that you have graced me to carry. What would you have us name her? Would you confirm it to the both of us so we can be sure that it is you speaking?"

She knew that the God who had given her this child also had a specific plan for this baby as promised in Jeremiah 1:5 and step one was her name. So, the young lady waited patiently for him to speak. Months went by.

A day came as she bathed herself in preparation for church one Sunday morning while on a visit at her parent's house. She sang quietly to herself not thinking about anything or anyone in particular. Her unborn baby seemed to kick more when she felt her mama having a bath. It was a beautiful sensation. Then she heard Him:

"Tiia. Tiiana" She smiled and said the name to herself over and over again.

"Mama Tiiana. Mama Tiia. Mama T." She played with the title that would be a lifelong badge of honour. She had asked God to confirm it right? She kept it to herself and did not share it with a single soul. God had to honour her request! Later that evening she received a text from 179.9 miles away.

"I've been looking at some names for our baby & these are the top 5 that I like. I feel strongly about & particularly drawn to the first one on the list though."

She silently read the first name. It said ***Tiia.***

Receiving Tiiana's name from the Lord at the time that I did, gave me a fresh level of strength that I had not been able to tap into so far during my pregnancy. That was my gift from the Lord because it represented so much more than a name. It spoke of hope, strength, a future, a turn around one day, comfort and most importantly His presence in my then present. Things had begun to move in an onwards and upwards direction in terms of my relationship with God but it was still a battle, just one I was now winning.

I even remember one Sunday breaking down in tears in the presence of my parents because I was afraid that my baby would either die in the womb or come out still born as a punishment from God for fornicating. It was such an irrational fear but a fear nonetheless.

As my parents ministered to me on the day I shared it with them, my heart came to a still and peace overwhelmed me however what sealed the deal for me was the day God told us what to name our daughter. To go out of His way to tell us what to name her gave me the assurance I needed to know that in spite of the conditions surrounding her entrance into this world as well as my own personal failings - God's hand was surely upon her. Why name someone you don't have plans for? God had heard me. God still heard me. I was reassured that God was with me and my child and that though difficult, we were going to get through this storm and look back one day and smile in gratitude. Oh, the treasure it is to know and hear the voice of God!

Another battle I faced was trying to maintain my joy and excitement about my unborn child while being condemned daily for getting pregnant with her in the first place. Babies are sensitive to their mother's emotions even from the womb and so it was paramount for me to guard my atmosphere – something that proved to be a difficult task as the weeks rolled by. It was already a horrible thing to feel ashamed of myself without the assistance of anyone else and with the direction that things were going I could have released a strong spirit of rejection over my child.

As difficult as things were in that season, I was alert enough to know that she was a perfect gift from God no matter what. I desperately needed my emotions to catch up with my head knowledge though. The baby shopping helped and endless hours of watching pregnancy and motherhood shows on my iPad but I needed something more. Something lasting. I knew that the enemy had already waged a fierce war against her from the womb and he would try any access point possible to get at her. This is was we are reminded in Ephesians 4:27 NIV to *"...not give the devil a foothold..."* Satan had lost the abortion battle as I determined to do the right thing by keeping her and so he now had to find another strategy. His aim was for me to go through my pregnancy hating my unborn child, blaming her for my pain and ultimately releasing the spirit of rejection over her from the womb so that she could live a life of rejection and never be able to fulfill her destiny.

Many women who have failed to connect emotionally with their children as they should, can trace the start of this issue to what they went through when they were pregnant with that particular child. When they should have been enjoying their unborn baby's kicks and turns, they were crying in a corner somewhere instead. The very hands that should have caressed their womb, shoulders and feet were weapons of violence towards them instead. When they should have been happily looking forward to the arrival of their baby their trimesters were filled with dread and sorrow. All of these things sowed seeds not only in them but in their unborn baby's life and without serious prayer and divine intervention from God, a rejected pregnant woman always results in a rejected child.

This was a fight I refused to lose. After my season of crying and feeling sorry for myself, it was now time to arise and fight. I still had breath in my body therefore victory was still for the taking. An extra reason to live had now been added to my life in the form of my unborn child but it could only be powered by prayer. Staying down and out could only have been an option if time was going to pause and wait for me and my emotions to be on the same page – but it wasn't. The ministry of motherhood was calling. Purpose was calling. And not a struggle form of motherhood full of bitterness & trying to prove a point to the world. No. A motherhood full of the life, light & love of God. After all Christ came *"that they may have life, and that they may have it more abundantly" (John 10:10).* This could only be brought into full manifestation by prayer & a strong relationship with God.

I knew all too well the story of Jabez which can be found in the book of 1 Chronicles 4:9-10. Jabez had to go before God in order to reverse the path of life his mother had set him on through the name she chose to give him. She transferred her pain and sorrow onto him even though he was innocent and not to blame for any of it. Had he not prayed and cried out to God then his life would have surely taken the course of pain. He would have lived to fulfil the curse spoken over his life. He had to undo the evil of the previous generation by making his request specific: *"that you would keep me from evil, that I may not cause pain!"* Personally, I refused for my daughter to have to fight a battle against a spirit I should have defeated in my time.

It didn't matter what I was going through as I carried her. It was not her fault. She was not going to ever have to pay for my anguish or rejection. She was a gift and I made sure to remind her as well as myself daily. As things improved in my spiritual life, I even began writing a journal to her that I will give her as a gift one day. I wrote prayers and dreams in there for her and told her just how much I loved her and couldn't wait to meet her. I laid hands on my belly and prophesied. I spoke the Word of God over what I was yet to fully behold and see with my own 2 eyes. I was not going to partner with the enemy in cursing and rejecting my child! There was a God who was more than capable of healing my broken heart & freeing me to walk in my calling as a mother in total wholeness.

Do you know how many people's lives are cursed and at a stand still because of evil words spoken over them when they were in their mother's womb? Because nobody reversed those words and prayed unto the Lord, those words currently have the final say in their lives and are determining the course of their destiny. Nothing seems to work out. Failed relationships after relationships. They can't keep money or do anything substantial with it and it always seems to run out no matter how much they make. They face rejection everywhere that they go and they have no peace. Someone somewhere along the line declared evil over them, whether out of anger, disappointment or shame and they are having to pay for something that is not their fault.

We must be careful of the things we speak when we are angry and overwhelmed. The Bible says: *"death and life are in the power of the tongue, and those who love it will eat of its fruit" (Proverbs 18:21).* Your world is shaped and determined by the confession of your mouth. Even God, when He created the world, used His mouth to call things into existence. We have that same creative power. Don't allow a temporary situation to lead you to confess things that will create permanent negative realities in your world.

God can turn around any situation and use it for good when it is fully surrendered to Him. When we lay aside our desire to fight and defend our name, reputation and simply allow Him to take control He shows up and shows out. He comes in confirming that He is with you and that you are not alone. After the pain, the disappointment, the mistake, the loss and whatever else you may face – there is a reason to live and carry on and that is what you must contend for in the presence of the Lord not as though your life depends on it but BECAUSE your life depends on it. A girl can lose many things but she will always have the power of prayer available to her and little by little I found my voice.

Just as I was given her name. God as a name to give you too no matter the bleakness of your current circumstances, if you will lean into His arms enough and tune into to hear His heartbeat you will realise that it beats for you and it speaks to you. The name He may give you to reassure and strengthen you might b: Forgiven, Unashamed, Accepted, Restored, Redeemed, Cleansed, Loved, Freed Cherished, Wanted, Healed or Uncondemned. A name that will minister to every last one of your pains, wounds and insecurities and cause them to melt away at the mention of the Word He has spoken over your life. A name that means how people see you and what they say about you genuinely stops controlling and ruling your life. A name given by the name that is above ever other name: Jesus. God has something to say to you, it is your duty to find out what. And for a reminder of many of the names He calls you by, read the back of the bookmark that came with this book.

I am going to share with you how I prayed over my daughters' life while she was in my womb and also how I still continue to pray over her & her brothers (Yes, I am a proud Mum of 2 now!) daily. I would pray at night, in the shower, out and about on walks and at any given opportunity I could find. There is no demon in hell that can withstand the power that is released when a mother goes to the war room for her children. None. If you don't pray – nobody else will. Now your specific situation may not be pregnancy related but you best believe that it is prayer dependant. There is nothing that will not respond to the power of prayer.

The most important prayer point out of everything I prayed concerning my child was one of dedication. I gave her to God and dedicated my unborn child to God from the womb, before any church service, ceremony or man of God ever prayed for her. I prayed for her. I declared that she would be a covenant child and made a deal with God that if I did my part of raising her in Him, for Him and with Him – ensuring that she was not a regular child who was allowed to watch & wear anything and everything as well as go & be found anywhere and everywhere then He had to keep His end of preserving her, filling her with a hunger for His presence and using her for His glory in a spectacular way.

Of course, as a mother it is impossible for me to be everywhere my children will be 24/7 and to be honest with you God never intended us to be a form of CCTV in our children's lives. That is the spirit of control and highly demonic. Our duty is to do our part in paving a godly way, setting the boundaries & teaching our children the ways of the Lord but above all to ensure that an altar of prayer is maintained consistently from the moment they are in our womb till the day we as parents leave this Earth.

A mother's prayers will always be able to reach where her hands and eyes can't. My children may outrun me but they can't outrun God. The Bible says in Proverbs 15:3: *"The eyes of the Lord are in every place, keeping watch on the evil and the good."* There is a God who can snatch, grab, fix & change anything and anyone on any corner of the globe if there is someone who simply avails themselves to pray. You cannot be a controlling mother and a prayerful mother.

I have seen many mothers put pressure on men of God to pray for their children who seem to suddenly become rebellious and wayward in their teen or young adult years. The things of God are not magic they are governed by principles. Where there has been no altar of prayer erected in the family by the parent(s) since that child was born – a parents first move needs to be one of repentance and taking responsibility for not playing the part God told them to play in their child's life from day one not demanding a man of God to magically fix something that was allowed to develop over the past 18 years or so. The prayer of a man of God can do nothing in an area where a proper foundation was not set and this applies in every area of your life: marriage, business, education, health and more. Repentance is your starting point.

"Train up a child in the way he should go, And when he is old he will not depart from it" (Proverbs 22:6). Church and Bible study are nice but they are to be an addition to what stems from the family home. The church cannot fix what was planted in your child due to a lack of prayer, godliness & boundaries in your house. No amount of anointing oil will cover up the fact that your child is allowed to watch television shows of violence, monsters and sexual activities. Sow the right seeds as early as possible so you can always quote God when the enemy tries to come knocking at any point. It is a guarantee that the very least the enemy will do is to try. Motherhood is a great responsibility

and a lifelong call. If you don't pray, your children and anything else entrusted into your care will become certain prey.

THE PAST ***(2 Corinthians 5:17, Isaiah 43:19, Hebrews 12:24)***

1. My baby shall not repeat any of the mistakes as well as sins made by me and her father, including having an out of wedlock pregnancy in Jesus name.
2. I break every generational curse, ungodly family pattern and evil cycle still at work in my bloodline **list them by name** and her father's bloodline **list them by name** in Jesus name. It ends with us and shall not cross over into her life in Jesus name.

THE PRESENT ***(Isaiah 54:17, Exodus 12:13, 1 Peter 2:9, Isaiah 59:19, Psalm 127:3)***

3. I cancel the assignment of the spirit of rejection over her life in Jesus name.
4. I render everything negative that was released over her life the day it was strongly suggested I abort her, powerless & destroyed with the blood of Jesus.
5. I destroy the assignment of the spirit of death and premature death against her life in Jesus name.
6. I break the rights and rulership o the spirits of anger, rage & violence that would have tried to find a home in her each time I was physically assaulted during my pregnancy.

7. I speak to you and tell you that you are loved, needed, wanted and accepted. You are not an accident but a covenant child in Jesus name.
8. I pray against any evil spirits that are sent to attach themselves to children conceived out of wedlock in Jesus name.
9. You shall not come our still born neither shall there be any complications surrounding your birth in Jesus name.

THE FUTURE ***(Joshua 24:15, John 16:8, Deuteronomy 28:13, 1 Corinthians 15:33, Luke 2:52, Numbers 6:24-27, Psalm 127:5)***

1. I pray for a definite day when the Holy Spirit will convict you of your sin and you will give your life to Christ with no backsliding or rebellion in Jesus name.
2. I pray that you will know the voice of God for yourself and walk intimately with Him in Jesus name.
3. I pray that you will discover your God given purpose, walk in it boldly and influence your generation for Jesus Christ in an immense way in Jesus name.
4. I pray that you would be the head and not the tail as well as a leader and not a follower of the crowd in Jesus name.
5. I pray that you will never succumb to peer pressure, join a gang or suffer from addiction. You will make godly friendship choices in Jesus name.
6. I pray for your education, studies and your mind. I declare that the spirit of excellence that was within Daniel is also within you. You will not fail, struggle to comprehend or repeat a class/exam in Jesus name.
7. I cover your virginity and sexuality in the blood of Jesus and declare it preserved until your wedding day. You will not jump from relationship to relationship in Jesus name.

I place the mark of the blood of Jesus upon you and declare that you are hidden from the sight of all timewasters in Jesus name.

8. I pray for your menstruation cycle and declare a pain free cycle for you in Jesus name. You will not have irregular periods in Jesus name.
9. I pray against barrenness of the womb in Jesus name. at the appointed time you shall bear children with ease and without any complications in Jesus name.
10. I pray for your future husband and pray for a man that is full of the fear of God in Jesus name. I pray for a man who will bring your closer to Christ, a man who will have fully left and cleaved unto you, who will honour you and raise your children in a godly manner. You shall not be drawn to cheaters, liars or physical /verbal abusers in Jesus name neither shall you divorce in Jesus name.

The above are some of the prayer points I prayed for my child and continue to pray for my children. The options are endless and I encourage you to add many more of your own as the Holy Spirit leads you. It is also important to pray for yourself as a parent. I believe that there is a generation that focused a lot on praying for their children to not bring them shame or be a "disgrace to the family" and never took adequate time to pray for themselves and for God to help them as parents. Hence, we have a generation that never apologised, thanked or congratulated their children as well as failed to verbally affirm them and firmly believed that a parent is always right. Parents who abused their children in the name of *"I am the parent"* and carried out gross injustices that have left many scarred and wounded for life. Listen, without the help of God: YOU WILL FAIL YOUR

CHLDREN and ultimately the God who chose you as their custodian. Without Him, I will fail in my assignment too. Wisdom is not automatic – it is a gift from God. *"If any of you lacks wisdom, let him ask of God, who gives to all liberally and without reproach, and it will be given to him" (James 1:5).* And so, I prayed and prayed, day in and day out, like a crazy unstoppable woman.

----- CHAPTER EIGHT -----

US VS. THE WORLD

Me and my fiancé would like to first and foremost thank God for His indescribable love and mercy towards us in what has been a life-changing season.

Next comes the blessing of family and friends and the safety net it has been for us as we have walked this journey. They have been instrumental in providing the atmosphere of peace we have so greatly needed.

To our local Pastors Mr & Mrs Dewah, we can't thank and honour you enough for showing us the firmness as well as love that parents ought to show their children. The church discipline process we underwent, the much-needed months of sit out time from ministry you instructed us to take as well as our weekly pre-marital counselling sessions have shaped us.

AFM Vessels of Honour – our church family. Thank you for supporting us and standing by us.

As Christians and lovers of Jesus we acknowledge that conceiving a child out of wedlock is a sin. We did sin and we recognise that what we did was very wrong and is wrong. There is no excuse. We are sorry. On top of being children of God we are also ministers therefore there is an example we are called to uphold and live by hence we feel the importance of coming openly before you to apologise and say that we are genuinely sorry for failing to do so.

The two of us love each other very much and are happy that we are still standing together by the grace of God in spite of our fights, disagreements and personal shortcomings which you can only imagine have been intensified during this past season. A threefold chord is not easily broken and we have quickly mastered that the victory is in fighting together and not each other as the enemy wishes.

With all of that being said, we are beyond excited to meet our precious princess and gift from God. Our joy is indescribable! In a short space of time we will officially be Mr & Mrs C. both by tradition and law – with our white wedding to come later on. We ask for your heartfelt prayers. God Bless You.

I remember the day we drafted the statement above word for word just as you have read it a few weeks before I gave birth. We posted it on our individual Facebook & Instagram pages for the public to see. We had driven to a quiet spot overlooking the city that we lived in one day and had began to pen down what we felt the Lord was leading us to share with His people regarding our situation. I wasn't sure what to expect to be perfectly honest with you but I was sure that this was the leading of the Lord and we both agreed. So, we joined hands, prayed and began to write.

We could have decided to say absolutely nothing as many others before us have done however we had to obey the leading of the Lord. I am a firm believer that when God has entrusted you to lead His people as well as placed you in a position of influence, while you don't have to explain absolutely everything that you do to them, there are some things of grave magnitude that you do. For us, a whole baby out of wedlock was one of them. I am glad we obeyed God.

"Behold, to obey is better than sacrifice" (1 Samuel 15:22). makes it clear that God prizes our obedience to Him over outward works. Had we ignored the leading of the Lord and gone on to carry on ministry as normal, preaching, singing & leading (sacrifices) we would have greatly displeased the Lord. God is not a toddler who you can distract with other more appealing toys, foods or games when He is waiting on you with a clear expectation or instruction. There is nothing more appealing to God than obedience. Obey.

The Shammah I was by the time we shared our news from our own lips with the world compared to the Shammah I was when the news was spilt behind our back without our consent were two completely different people. I still had areas inside of me that needed healing but I had come a long way and concerning this particular decision that we made, I was filled with the strength of the Lord. I felt a peace because I knew I was doing what was pleasing to the Lord. People could react how they wanted because I knew that I was once again in right standing with God and I had a secret place to retreat to, not as a stranger but as a son should anything try to shake my faith.

The Word of God says: *"there is therefore now no condemnation to those who are in Christ Jesus, who do not walk according to the flesh, but according to the Spirit" (Romans 8:1).* The key is being IN Christ. Not just with Him, or around Him because that is not good enough. You must immerse yourself in Him, His presence, His Word & His passions as a lifestyle. You will never receive the freedom you need if you have one foot in and the other foot out. Neither will the weight of what you carry ever completely lift if you are determined to hold onto a portion of it. God can be trusted. He has never returned a load or heavy burden back to the one who completely surrenders it to Him so if you are still feeling it, you have not completely let go. Once He takes it – it is completely gone. So, what's stopping you? The memories of what happened, what they did, said and didn't do? He is more than enough for all of that. Get in Him.

When I looked at my phone some hours after our public statement I was gobsmacked. My personal inboxes were overflowing with messages from females who were telling me that seeing our post had given them the courage to go through with their pregnancy and not abort their unborn baby. Others shared stories of their own rejection and ostracisation from family, friends and the church and their realisation that it was time to forgive and start a fresh page with God. Many were touched, inspired and encouraged to never try to save their reputations by using two wrongs to make a right. The post literally went viral. The testimonies that came from us sharing our story were endless and to this day continue to reach my personal inboxes. I wept in worship that day and for many days to come. What a good God!

Who could have thought that the Lord would use my once guilt, shame and condemnation to lift His name so highly like that? Who knew my story would be the catalyst many females needed to finally begin a healing process they had perhaps been avoiding for years? Who would have thought that restoration would take place in families as people were convicted of their wrong handling of their loved one's sins? Who could have known that trusting and honouring God in a tunnel that had seemed to have no end to it would inspire others to do the same in all areas of their lives? Who would have known lives would be rededicated to Christ? Who would have known people would have finally been able to cry tears they never got the chance to release and pour out words, emotions and thoughts they had never had a person to share them with? Who could have known that God would take what the enemy meant for evil and turn it into something oh so good? Obedience pays!

The greatest testimony however was that after all of the messages and the phone calls of encouragement and admiration that I received that day, what I looked forward to the most was the conversation of thanksgiving I promised to have with the Lord later that evening before bed. It was like a woman looking forward to a date with her lover. Yes, the day is full of many happenings, conversations & interactions but the focus of her heart and the song of her soul is the fact that she gets to spend quality time with the one that has captured her heart. The closing of distance between two lovers and the fact that after all was said and done my heart once again truly longed for Him & His presence above everything else was the real glory. There is nothing like being restored back to the One you love. There is nothing like missing communion with the One you love and knowing that it is not just a wish anymore but a craving that can be filled there and then because guilt, shame & condemnation have finally lost all of their false rights of mediation. To have my prayer life back again is what I cherished the most & to know that instead of discarding me and my shame, God chose to prove a point to the enemy and that is that He is the One that has the final say.

I remember a few weeks after getting married, I received a few messages along the lines of *"Congrats sis. At least all things worked together for your good because the two of you ended up getting married anyway."* My response was and still is the same: All things worked together for my good because God got the glory from my story and salvation was brought to many. Also understand that no matter the amount of people that were there for me during my pregnancy it didn't stop the spiritual attacks from happening. There are some demons you have to confront by yourself and a man by your side is not an escape from that reality. Yes, getting married was a blessing but getting married did not cover my shame. The blood of Jesus is what covered my shame. The finished work of the Cross is what covered my shame. The nail pierced hands are what covered my shame. The crown of thorns is what covered my shame. The One who hung on the Cross bearing my fornication is what covered my shame. Jesus covered my shame. At any point of my story that

I chose God over myself and over other people, no matter the consequences: things were working together for my good.

But I know there is a woman reading this who is struggling to accept the reality of being a single mother and the fact that the father of the child she carries could not, did not and would not stand by her. A woman who was just as guilty as the man for committing the sin of fornication but is pained because it seems the man easily escaped responsibility because after all he is not the one who will carry the child. I know a woman sees no light at the end of the tunnel or an end destination where the song of her soul will be *"Indeed, all things worked together."*

The shame of disappointing your parents and loved ones hangs over you like an itch that won't go away because this was not how it was supposed to turn out. There should have been a celebration, a joining of two families and the beginning of a life long secure union to raise your child under. You wonder and question why you could not have a happy ending like the other women you know and especially the ones you see on the gram and the pain seems unbearable. You envision the way people will look at you as you walk into a room with your growing bump or growing child and know it will break you as they scan your hand to see if there is a ring there, though you may never show a public sign.

You worry about coping, providing, balancing & managing. You are concerned about how your child will be affected by a broken home and whether you will ever be mum enough for the voids and places that surely only a father can fill. You can't reconcile the brokenness of your current season and the beautiful ending that myself and so many others claim exists. It hurts and you want it to stop at any cost. You. Can't. Do. This.

I have counselled so many women over the years and have been on the listening and advising end of so many marital issues especially when the foundation was a baby that inspired an overnight marriage for the purpose of public damage control.

Do you know that there exists a wife who cries herself to sleep at night while her husband is next to her on his phone gleefully texting other women? However, the gram only shows you the matching outfits that cover the ever-gaping hole in her heart that only God can fill. Do you know that there is a woman who is accustomed to receiving violent blows from her husband's hands while her innocent child watches? But in public the way he holds and kisses her in front of you inspires you to even ask God for a similar kind of man. There is a wife whose heart begins to beat at the speed of lightning and whose palms sweat when she hears her husbands car pull up or the key in the door begins to turn because she doesn't know which version of him is returning back home that day or night. Check Facebook though and you will see beautiful statuses of devotion for each other that give you hope for tomorrow yet she is in desperate need of the safety & protection that only Abba can give.

There is a woman who is last place in her home as relatives and family continually dictate the pace, temperature & climate of her home and her husband silently or vocally allows it with no regard for her. But on Valentines Day she is the one and only as well as the first and the last. Do you know that there is a wife whose husband calls her and their children indescribable scarring names each time his anger is aroused?

Yet the smiles you see give the impression that all is well in paradise. Do you know that there is a wife who is not affirmed, hugged or kissed because the husband married her out of a sense of cultural duty – nothing more and nothing less. He makes love to his other women and so she rocks herself to sleep at night unaware that God is waiting arms extended to soothe the rejection. However, you are sure a man would fix all of your problems and current dilemma.

There is a woman whose part time job involves stalking her husbands gadgets, accounts and communications to keep herself quietly updated on who his latest side-chick is so she can use that information to try to make adjustments on herself by any means necessary and hopefully cause him to stop the unending infidelity. But you'd never know that because they are goals. Do you know there is a woman who lives in major regret wishing she had chosen the path of a single mother earlier in life and not used marriage as an escape from shame because shame has still managed to locate her dwelling place and build extra rooms there?

There is a wife who goes through the torture of her husband accidentally and repeatedly mentioning the names of other women during their time of intimacy as well as repeatedly denying that He is stepping out on her in any way, shape or form leaving her broken and confused. Do you know that there is a wife who was once full of light, love & passion for God and everything around her but is now an empty shell of a being because of being joined to a husband who did not have the capacity to lead her? A woman who is so bitter at her current reality she does not have the capacity or willingness to respect her husband. It is tit for tat and she willingly allows venom to spew from her mouth because that is the only way she can see to defend herself and pretend she is a strong *insert race here* woman. There is a wife whose husband must masturbate before and after her because she will never be good enough & the rush into marriage meant the counselling that would have brought the spirit of lust to the surface was rushed or skipped altogether.

You were not rejected sis. You were protected. You were not forsaken sis. You were covered by God. You were not abandoned sis. You were actually given another chance. A marriage will not cover up a shame that you have not allowed Abba to cover up neither is pressure a solid foundation to begin a marriage union on. His early exit from your life means that you can recover earlier on in your journey instead of attempting to recover from his exit in the form of a divorce years later when you have sacrificed every single thing you have to your name. Your time. Your money. Your self-esteem. Your child. Your confidence. Your friends. Your family. Your dreams. Your aspirations. Your purpose.

It is better to go through a few intense and painful years of walking with God amidst ridicule, shame & gossip as a single mother while He prepares you for a man that will love, cherish and honour you according to God's original blueprint of what a husband is supposed to be. A man from God. A man of God. A man like Christ. It will not always be like this. I repeat, you were not rejected sis… you were protected. Let she that has ears to hear... Hear.

I encourage you to view whatever you may be going through as a long road and at the end of that road picture a destination called "ALL THINGS WORKING TOGETHER." Live life with the consciousness that everything you do for the genuine glory of God and in total obedience to Him is a step closer towards that destination. It doesn't matter how hard it is or how tough it is – it is possible to obey God and there is a reward. Also remember that everything you do that chooses the devil over God is also a step backwards from that destination of a good outcome. What will you choose today?

Was everyone ministered to? Inspired? Encouraged? In support? Of course, not but neither did we hold ourselves accountable to the people so they could give us a round of applause or fall into agreement with us. We did it in obedience to the Father's leading. Again, the Bible says: *"behold, to obey is better than sacrifice" (1 Samuel 15:22).* In fact, one particular young lady went onto social media and did a live video stream which received hundreds and possibly thousands of views talking about what we had done and how disappointed she was. Understandable. I remember being mocked, called names & ridiculed but like I said, the Shammah after the storm was not the same Shammah prior to the storm. She had encountered Love. So, I went into the presence of the Lord and poured out my heart to Him. My heart and my hurt. It hurt me because we had once had a friendship where I spent a Christmas at her house with her family and though we had grown distant we had kept in communication but this forgiven girl was now determined to be a girl after the Lord's heart and so I forgave her knowing that the goodness of God would forever in a million years outweigh the evil of man.

There is a saying that goes: *"Forgiveness is setting a prisoner free, only to realise that the prisoner was you."* And another saying goes: *"Holding onto unforgiveness is like drinking poison and expecting the other person to die."* The truth in these statements is life changing. You are the one who suffers the most when you hold onto the things people did against you. You cannot call your journey a testimony when you are still bitter against the people who made you suffer at any point during your journey. When you allow God to refine you completely you see everything and everyone as a blessing no matter what happened because you understand that you probably wouldn't be as close to God as you are if they hadn't played their part in your story. We read of Jesus saying, *"Father, forgive them, for they do not know what they do" (Luke 23:34).* It is not because what they did to Him was right – it was because His heart was bent on pleasing the Father no matter what. Forgive. It is what the Father would have you do because He forgave you. Let go. It's what God would have you do because His Son did the same when He hung innocently on a Cross for you. Release them. It's what Jesus did for you.

During the writing of this book as I was about halfway through, a test came my way. One of the individuals who had a front row, silent and enabling seat to the abuse I went through when pregnant contacted me. It was the first time I had a clear opportunity to address any of the things that ever happened and in typical *"I need closure"* fashion, I took the leap and had an exchange of words that left me feeling drained & burdened. Let's just say that I rightfully divided the word of truth & receipts unto them but instead of the peaceful feeling one should feel when they get something off their chest, I felt heavy and so I took myself to the presence of the Lord and began to pray. I should have denied the invitation to converse completely but the upside was it showed me everything within me that was still tender from my pregnancy. The Lord highlighted to me that wholeness is a journey that is made up of various healings. He had healed my heart of certain things but I was on a lifelong journey of allowing Him to mould me and work in me and fix every last hurtful place within.

He showed me that every place within me that would ever get triggered even if it was just an inch was not something for me to beat myself up about or begin that downward spiral towards condemnation-ville but rather it simply gave me and Him more to talk about in the prayer room. Loads in fact. He reminded me that the focus of the Christian race was not to outrun, outdo or overtake those in nearby lanes but to stay the course of my own lane and hand in hand with Him navigate the hurdles and get back up again if I tripped over any.

The way I was triggered that day gave the enemy an opportunity to whisper, *"Ha! So that little part of you is still tender… well – that's a fail. Probably best to cancel the idea of this book altogether mate…"* but God's way of saying *"No. I instructed you to write that book. Write. The trigger means the conversation we have been having for years is not yet over and that's okay. Let's keep talking and I will keep working on you."* The parts of you that still hurt are not a sign that you are a failure nor that you are a hopeless case, they are a personalised invitation from Jesus for you to have conversation with Hm. A conversation that will transform your life, heal your world and catapult you into a place you could have never dreamed possible. So while it is not His will for anyone to bleed while they lead – there comes a time when He has done a type of work within you that He wants you to testify of even if according to your own reasoning it would be "better"'if circumstances were slightly different or if you felt more superhuman. His Word says, *"And He said to me, "My grace is sufficient for you, for My strength is made perfect in weakness." Therefore, most gladly I will rather boast in my infirmities, that the power of Christ may rest upon me" (2 Corinthians 12:9).*

He reminded me how the Bible says God is a *"rewarder of those who diligently seek Him" (Hebrews 11:6)* as well as the promise in Jeremiah 29:13 which says: *"And you will seek Me and find Me, when you search for Me with all of your heart."* There is no greater reward than Him. In essence all of our hurts should drive us to the presence of the Lord to the point where we find Him and encounter His presence and glory in a fresh way. He showed me how those who continue to struggle with unforgiveness are those who have not sought Him deep enough and spent time in His presence long enough – why? Because if they had, they would have found Him and it is impossible to truly encounter God and still be mad at the people and the situations that drove you to find Him in the first place.

It's a journey & He is with you every step of the way. Refuse to speak, sing or share without His say so just because you feel it is the right thing to do so or it seems to be the trend to share heart breaking and capturing stories before an audience of some sort. The spirit in which you do a thing is what ministers and not the thing that you do. But sis, the very day, hour & second that our beloved Abba releases you to indeed speak, sing & share in whatever form He directs you to .. roar Daughter of Zion… Roar.

It's not the time to call your friends to re-discuss what that person said and did to you. It's time to run into the welcoming arms of Jesus. It is not the time to post subliminal messages on your social media so that the person who wronged you sees it. It's time to run into the safe arms of Jesus. It's not time to devise a strategy of revenge to get back at that person so you can make them feel what they made you feel. It's time to run into the loving arms of Jesus. He understands you in a way that nobody else will ever be able to and He is able to give you comfort and peace for every one of your troubles.

God's requirement for us to forgive is not Him dismissing our pain or saying that whatever happened to us is not important – it's Him reminding you that your relationship with Him is more important. Through the pain He is able to give you all of the strength you need to release what happened. Mention their names through the tears and the lump in your throat and the tightness in your chest and tell Abba that you forgive them. Every last one of them for every last thing they did. Your emotions will get the memo later but you can decide today & right now because true healing can only be found in Him and so I encourage you to make the choice to forgive and never look back.

Dear Lord, again I bring Your precious child before you. They are going to speak to you in a moment in their own words and way but I want to stand in the gap for them for a moment. For you to require them to forgive even after the level of pain, rejection & hardship that they have gone through at the hands of people who chose not to fear You it must mean there is a perspective You have that we don't have. Lord I ask that you give them that perspective as well as peace right now in the name of Jesus. For the closure they think they need but have not gotten and will never get please show them that your presence is all of the closure they will ever need. Take away the sting of their storm and the burden of what broke them. Help them to forgive. Help them to let it go. Help them to release every last word, look, action & wound that threatened to see them finished for good. Help them to forgive the tears they had to cry & the coping mechanisms they developed as a result of the pain which in turn snatched them further and further away from you. Help them to forgive it all. Take their hand because they can't do it without You. Above all wrap them in your arms and remove the bitterness at the breaking and the process of becoming. In Jesus precious name I pray for them. Amen. **Your turn.**

----- CHAPTER NINE -----

TIME TO PUSH!

"Yoooooooooooooooooooooo!" The young lady exclaimed as she woke up abruptly from her sleep. She looked at the time. It was just after 1am and the pain that had woken her up was nothing like the Braxton Hicks she had been experiencing for the past few weeks. No sir! This particular jolt of pain surpassed them all, by far. This had to be it!

She remembered how she had obsessed for months on how she would truly know for sure that she was in labour. She didn't want to miss it and just suddenly pop out her baby in the supermarket or some other public place. She wanted to be ready, prepared and in control. Her loved ones had laughed at her in a friendly manner and assured her that when the time was right, she would KNOW. They repeatedly explained to her that there would be no mistaking the real contractions for false ones when they came. How right they were! The young lady quickly sent a text.

"Our baby is definitely coming today. The pain I just felt. I know it's today!" She tried to relax and go back to sleep as excitement quietly bubbled up from inside her.

The next day the pain increased. The young lady maintained her composure and rocked herself back and forth through the contractions as her labour progressed. She played worship music in the background while nibbling on pineapples and reminding herself that every contraction was one contraction closer to having her beautiful baby in her arms.

"Keep calm!" She told herself repeatedly. She was taking her own advice well! Then another unexpected jolt came. Nope. Calm could get out of the window. She had to get to the hospital NOW!

Hours later the young girl huffed, puffed & screamed the labour ward down as her baby girl drew ever nearer to being born. She paced, squatted, breathed & hummed. Thank God for her birthing partner. She had done well by going without any pain relief for 20hours of her labour until she finally had to ask for something to relieve the pain. She had to have something.

"Gooooooooooooooooood!" She screamed and called on His Mighty Wonder Working Name as she pushed and tried to leap off the bed at one point. The midwife began shouting.

"The head! I see the head! Shammah push!" Suddenly but all in a split second, it was as though everyone in the room ceased to be there. It was her and the assignment at hand. It was her and what she had been entrusted to birth. Her vs. Everything she had gone through for the past 9 months to ensure she did not reach this day. Her vs. The sleepless nights. Her vs. The cravings, aches and pains. Her vs. The tears. Her vs. The abuse. Her vs. The rejection. But her God vs. Them. Her God. The only reason she had survived. She could do this. She could. She had come so far. She could do it! One last agonising, sweat breaking & excruciating push as gloomy grey ashes were turned into undeniable beauty & months of deep silent sorrow suddenly became undiluted joy... The baby arrived.

Every single sermon I had ever heard where the preacher used an anecdote or metaphor of a woman's labour to explain a point finally made sense the day I gave birth to my daughter. It's one thing to know something because of scientific head knowledge – it's another thing all together to experience it first-hand. It really is true that the closer you are to your blessing, the tougher and almost unbearable things become. You become convinced that you are not going to be able to make it and that giving up is the only option that you have not knowing that if you would just hold on a little while longer – everything will make so much sense to the point that you forget you were ever in pain.

The moment I laid eyes on Tiia every single drop of pain disappeared from my body. Immediately. So, they hadn't been lying about that part. She was so beautiful and perfect. Her big eyes slowly trying to take in the new world all around her. Her small fingers clinging onto mine for dear life. I will never be able to adequately describe that precious moment and that's okay. I just cried and stared at her and cried and stared some more. She was finally here and by the grace of God, I had done it. If such a beautiful blessing was what lay on the other side of my pushing, sweating and intense breathing techniques – then it had all been worth it. Every mother reading these words has already travelled down memory lane because the day you see and hold your child for the first time is a moment that can never be erased from your mind. And to the woman that is pregnant and reading these words… the sight, sound & scent of your baby will be worth every page of your story.

This is a small picture of the kind of restoration God has to give you for your life, emotions, finances, confidence, strength and all the other areas of your life that have been affected by what you have gone through. When God is through with you – you will be able to rejoice genuinely from the very depths of your heart. What God wants to do in you and for you will be so beautiful, it will make you forget that you ever felt hopeless, rejected and broken once upon a time. His promise of giving you *"beauty for ashes, the oil of joy for mourning, the garment of praise for the spirit of heaviness..."* Isaiah 61. stands true and firm over your life. When God blesses and restores, He does a perfect job.

I am talking the true, deep restoration from the inside out where you don't have to pretend you are happy or go out of your way to paint a certain image on social media for people. Been there, done that. When God does it there are no traces or patches of what you went through for people to see. They themselves will be unable to deny that God did this. He even has this way of restoring you in the presence of those who were front row witnesses to your shame & your story. Psalm 23 style, *"You prepare a table before me in the presence of my enemies; You anoint my head with oil; My cup runs over" (Psalms 23:5).* All broken pieces are mended. All shame is wiped away. All condemnation is removed. All tears are transferred from sorrow to joy. His glory overshadows you and speaks for you.

We have to get tired of posting beautiful selfies that are really and truly only a mask for the tears we cried ourselves to sleep with just the night before. We have to stop pretending to be the life of the party for all to see when deep down we want to jump off a bridge and end it all. We have to stop being the perfect go to for everyone else while we have absolutely no one to go to. It has to stop. Now! The Father wants to make each one of us whole step by step, lesson by lesson & encounter by encounter. We don't have to live fake lives when there is a God who is eagerly waiting to restore us and put us back together again so we can live real lives. Get into His presence. Wait on Him. Cry out to Him. Endure in Him. Allow God to do the restoring in your life because you cannot restore yourself.

Entering into a new relationship will not bring about the restoration that your heart is truly yearning for. Getting married will not give you inner peace and joy. Money will not lift condemnation from your heart and mind. A new job, house or car will not heal the wounds that still cut you so deep or erase the painful memories. Only God can heal you. Only God can forgive you. Only God can transform your life.

Without endurance, there would have been no beautiful baby. I had to hold on – through ugly screams and horrendous shouts yes – but holding on, nonetheless. The Apostle Paul says to us in Hebrews 12:1, *"let us run with endurance the race that is set before us"* Your walk with God requires you to remain steadfast and focused. It is not about who can get there the quickest, it is about who lasts the longest. You will encounter many hurdles and obstacles along the way but remember to endure and keep your eyes fixed on Jesus. God would not tell us to endure if He did not have the strength to give us for the endurance. Like I just said, His Word says, *"My grace is sufficient for you, for My strength is made perfect in weakness" (2 Corinthians 12:9).* You will come out of what you are going through but you must endure.

I encourage you to push in prayer over your situation. It does not matter what has happened – God is waiting to hear from you. Did you know that prayer is what connects heaven and earth? 2 Chronicles 7:14 says, *"if My people who are called by My name will humble themselves, and pray and seek My face, and turn from their wicked ways, then I will hear from heaven, and will forgive their sin and heal their land."* The promise to bring healing to us is conditional because it is tied to whether or not you and I will pray. If you don't pray, you will not see the hand of God move on your behalf. Only those who push in pray are the ones who will see results at the end of the day.

You may feel like you have been praying for an eternity. PUSH! Discouragement may be coming your way from all directions. PUSH! The path ahead may seem so blurry that you don't even see a point in praying about it. PRAY! You may find that on some days you can pray and on others you *feel* like you can't do it. PUSH! The weight of condemnation may not have completely lifted over you yet. PUSH! Others around you may be doing what they want, how they want and when they want with no regard for God. PUSH! You may doubt the effectiveness of even bothering because you once strayed so far away from God. PUSH! No one around you may be in support of your decision to please God above all others. PUSH! People may be walking away from you, distancing themselves from you & acting funny because of your godly decision. PUSH! The enemy may be attacking your thoughts daily with thoughts of worthlessness and how you don't qualify for the new way you are trying to live. PUSH!

There are no tears of joy for those who don't persevere. There is no testimony for those who don't pass the test. There is no glory for those who refuse to allow God to be the one to write their story. Push friend, PUSH!

----- CHAPTER TEN -----

REFLECTIONS

My heart is filled with so much gratitude as I sit writing the end of this book. I now understand what David meant when he said in Psalm 126:1, *"When the Lord brought back the captivity of Zion, we were like those who dream."* There are certain realities & outcomes in Christ that are too beautiful for the human mind to comprehend and understand. Who am I that God would be so mindful of me? No, really... what about my twenty something years of life can I confidently point at as being some sort of qualification for this level of grace that I have received from God?

I know of many who have killed themselves by going through half of what I went through but here I am still living. I don't take it lightly. If I had never seen it before then I clearly see it now. It is absolutely nothing to do with my name, background, status, popularity, beauty or age. It is only because of His unending love for me and infinite mercies that I sit here writing to you today with both me and my daughter ALIVE. In the moments when Tiia gets extremely loud as she plays and I am temped to quieten her down rather brashly as the noise gets to my head I must always remember that it could have been a very different story. I could have had the so called peaceful and deathly quiet house only because it would have been built on the foundation of shedding innocent blood to save a reputation. I'm in love with Jesus! He is amazing.

I must strongly remind you that the Jesus who said to the woman caught in adultery in John 8, *"neither do I"* is the same Jesus who also commanded her to *"go and sin no more"* in the very same sentence. The level of grace and forgiveness He had extended towards her was not just for people to stop condemning her and killing her that day it was also divine empowerment for her to start living a brand-new life from that moment on. A life that would please Him and glorify Him with each waking moment. A life of no compromise. A life where the claim to be a follower of Christ would be consistently backed up by her attitude, dressing, motives, decisions & secret devotion life. A life of genuine and true surrender.

We must understand that God's grace is not to be taken for granted and that the only appropriate response to it is laying down our lives for Him. The price for all of Him is giving up all of us. In Romans 6:1 a sobering question is posed to us: *"What shall we say then? Shall we continue in sin that grace may abound? Certainly not! How shall we who dies to sin live any longer in it?"* You have a responsibility to live uprightly. As much as it is through the help of the Holy Spirit for one to live a sin-free life, that is not a getaway card for you to deliberately put yourself around temptation with the hope that God will sort everything out for you. It doesn't work that way.

Boundaries must still be maintained, the right company must still be kept, what you expose your body, ears, eyes & lips to must still be kept pure, ungodly relationships must still be cut off, self-control must still be exercised as well as all of the other fruits of the Spirit we read about in Galatians 5:22-23. Defend your relationship with God passionately through the daily decisions that you make. When you have been given such a wonderful second chance or the hundredth chance for some of us – make use of it with all that you have. I know I will.

If you do fall, run full speed to the presence of Jesus and sort out your issues immediately. Don't wait. Run to Him. He is your heavenly Father and we have to strengthen our relationships with Him to the point that when we fall we don't run in the opposite direction of where He is but rather, we sprint towards Him. Think of what a child does when they fall to the ground as they are walking, running and playing. The first person that comes to mind is mum or dad and they run and cry freely in their arms. The arms of your Heavenly Father are a safe place for your heart, mind, thoughts, fears and burdens to be released. There is no condemnation in His presence. There is no judgement. Just love. Run to Him.

Don't try to calculate your walk with God or apply logical reasoning. God will strengthen you and restore you in HIS own timing and not according to your schedule or the pressures that the people around you may be putting on you. All of our hearts are different because we all experience different things in this life. Take your eyes off people's faces and their expectations and look unto Jesus *"the authour and finisher of our faith" (Hebrews 12:2).* His timing is perfect His ways are perfect and He knows exactly what He is doing with you. Trust Him.

You are not lagging bchind – you are being hidden in the presence of the Lord. You are not missing out – you are being protected. God is the redeemer of time. *"I will restore to you the years that the swarming locust has eaten, the hopper, the destroyer, and the cutter, my great army, which I sent among you" (Joel 2:25).* So, get lost in God. Fill your days and moments with Him, His presence and His word. Seeking God is not a waste of time. Seeking God is what will break the chains of guilt, shame and condemnation off your life and lead you into true freedom.

There is no dark tunnel that does not have an end. Your situation might seem like you will never come out of it -but believe me, you are closer than you think. The God who is so deeply in love with you is not only present in your current situation – He is already present at your end destination and with Him everything will work out for your good.

Never forget that functioning does not equate to freedom. If you note earlier on in the book I mentioned the first time I was invited to minister and the first time I actually did minister. Those were two separate dates. I made the mistake of thinking I was now doing well and accepted a request to be one of the deliverance ministers during a revival service that was held not long after I gave birth to my baby. As the time came for me to minister alongside the other ministers, the host gave me the signal that it was time and I suddenly couldn't move. I literally froze and my legs would not walk towards the pulpit. My heart was beating so fast and I immediately became aware that it was still premature for me to minister though many months had passed. I simply shook my head and settled for assisting the ushers with covering the saints that fell under the power of God for the rest of the evening. There was no way I was going to engage in active deliverance lest Sons of Sceva Part 2 decided took place.

Though strengthening my relationship with God in private, I had not reached the point of overflow that would have enabled me to effectively minister to other people. So, I didn't, however I knew what to do this time. There was no guilt, no self-pity or wallowing for days and weeks on end in a self-centred distant-from-God bubble. I stayed in the presence of God spending time with Him not so I could run back to minister but because time with Him was worth it and will always be worth it.

Had I tried to force it on that day, I would have been functioning yes on the outside but bound on the inside. What would have been the point in that? I would have been able to deceive man but God sees right through me. Instead of allowing my fear and worries over whether or not I would ever become all God had originally called me to be and do, I went to the presence of the Lord and HE began restoring my identity, my sense of self-worth and my confidence in His promises over my life. It didn't happen overnight – it has taken many months of weeping in prayer before the Lord but it happened. Now I am free to boldly walk out my calling and live out my purpose. God's destiny for you still stands. You will still preach! You will still sing for God! You will still write those books! You will run that business! You will have a godly marriage! You will still fulfil purpose! You will still be used by God. YOU WILL! YOU WILL! YOU WILL!

Currently my prayer life consists of several prayer points that stem from my season of pregnancy with my daughter. I am very protective of my children however I always pray that the Lord helps me to strike an ongoing balance between operating from a place of wise boundaries versus a place of fear. I had to release the mum-guilt that came from the fact that I failed to stand up for myself and my child adequately during my pregnancy. Yes, I have seen the extent of evil human beings can boldly display but I refuse to live in a cave of fear and stifle my children's growth because of a season of pain I went through as their mother. Some days I get it right and other days not so much but I know that as long as I stay holding Abba's hand, He will never lead me astray.

I continually mention the names of those who mistreated me during my pregnancy before the Lord. I don't mention them just to half heartedly tick a heavenly register and say *"at least I did it."* I do it because God commands me to and thankfully as time has progressed He has shown me as well as reminded me of some of the childhood pains and traumas of the individuals that were at the root of some of the treatment I was given. And so, I pray. The human hearts is very interesting in the sense that you can go for years without feeling pain, shedding tears or harbouring painful memories then one day as you are walking and minding your business, you'll see a duck crossing the road and boom, something within you explodes and you feel as though whatever it is only took place that morning. I continually ask the Lord to search the deep, hidden places so there are no surprises. The wound you ignore or are unaware of today will wound you deeper tomorrow in the most inconvenient way, place and time.

I earnestly pray for my emotional bond with my children. I pray that it would blossom and produce godly generational fruit. During my daughters first developmental review, all of her results came back extremely high and excellent however her emotional development was slightly lower than the rest. They reassured me that it was nothing to worry about and gave me a very useful list of activities to do to continue to strengthen this area but for me it bothered my greatly. However, the Spirit of the Lord called me out of the pit of self-pity and as I spent time with Him he showed me a few thing.

He began to show me things such as how when playing with my daughter I could sometimes drift off into my own thoughts for a very long time without realising and reminisce the past while she continued to play by herself in silence in my presence. This was all valuable time I could be using to interact with her more. He showed me him I had drastically reduced the amount of times I talked to her (talking to children from conception aids their development even though they don't understand a word yet) since she was in my womb (we talked all day everyday back then). I found my voice back. He showed me one day how more often than not, my resting face was a serious frown even when there was nothing immediately wrong and how Tiiana began to copy that because children do what they see. God continued to reveal & I continued to change. See, the excuse of *"well they put me through hell so this I why I even have negative memories to dwell upon in the first place"* was not going to cut it. It was my responsibility to do something about where I was in that moment by surrendering to God. If you've ever seen me & Tiiana together now then you know that the bond is special. I know that it is because I serve a God who answers prayer. Prayers I will continue to make for as long as I have breath.

Above all, I pray that I may continue to grow in my love and knowledge of the Lord. I pray that I may never fail Him in the way that I did before the people He entrusted me to represent Him. My heart and mind opened to sin long before my legs did and so I must continually keep those areas surrendered to the Lord. I ask Him to keep me and to show me how to stay holding His hand no matter the twists and turns of life. I know now why the singer wrote 'I'd rather have Jesus, than silver and gold.' He is the most precious person that a woman can ever have in her life and for what He did for me I have vowed to serve Him for all of my days. Do you know what it is to be resurrected from the dead? I owe Him my life because He restored my identity. I owe Him my life because I get to spend eternity with Him once again. I owe Him my life because He did not replace me with another but gave me an undeserved millionth chance. Hear me, there is a way you must live when you know you could be dead. I belong to Him…

There are some who will forever refuse to acknowledge my calling because of what I did and that is okay – be prepared for the same too but also know that once God moves on – life can finally truly move on. The glory is not in re-gaining people's approval but in gaining your relationship with God back. I knew better, I didn't do better and God in is infinite mercy, still gave me better. When they are sure Christ will give them the go ahead to stone you He still responds to them all with the same statement:

"Let any of you who is without sin be the first to throw a stone at her."

No one qualifies to throw anything after that. No Pastor, no parent, no friend and certainly no enemy. If you would fix your eyes on Jesus you'll realise that He is all you need. Your condemners have no power over the love and freedom that you find in Christ. And as surely as the adulterous woman's condemners couldn't condemn her then – yours can't either. Who dares declare hopelessness wen Hope Himself embraces you in His arms? At His feet you find mercy and strength to go and sin no more. Strength to stand. The new name He gives you even if you should have known better, empowers you to go and sin no more.

So, even though we will never know her name, we know His name... Redeemer. Forgiver. Lover. Restorer. Abba.

It is my sincere prayer that through this book, every mislabelled person that has had their head bowed low in guilt, shame and condemnation is now finally able to raise it back up again towards Him. Towards Love. Towards Peace. Towards Strength. Towards Jesus, the only One in this entire universe with the certain right to throw the first, second and hundredth stone but instead continually chooses to whisper 3 of the most powerful words to have ever been said in history.

Neither Do I...

-

---- CHAPTER ELEVEN -----

GIFTED

GIFTED is a WhatsApp support group that the Lord let me to start after Tiiana was born. We are currently in its 3rd consecutive year. It is based on Psalm 127:3 which clearly tells us that ALL children are a GIFT from God. Regardless of how a child came about to be – God does not release children into a woman's womb by accident. He is a God of purpose therefore every woman that is carrying a child or has given birth to one is GIFTED.

It is for the expecting female and the woman with children beneath the age of 1. The hoard of testimonies I received awakened me to the reality that my story and journey is not the first of its kind and women, especially in the church are suffering in silence as they fail to receive the Christ like support they are supposed to receive after making a wrong turn. Even if a woman conceives in marriage often times she is forgotten about, sidelined & mistreated by relatives or in-laws. These women need a safe place to express themselves, cry out and be heard.

So, in GIFTED we cover each-other. It is a sisterhood founded upon the Word of God and we strongly believe in the power of prayer, fasting and warring for our children. I hope that the testimonies on the next few pages bless and encourage you as much as they do me each time I read them. They are from the group of mothers who were in the first year of GIFTED. It runs yearly and each year on Tiiana's birthday I start another WhatsApp group with mothers from across the world.

In **year 1** we had 22 mothers from 8 different countries, there were 9 births (5 boys and 2 girls) and also 2 marriages by the grace of God. In **year 2** we had 17 mothers from 4 different countries, there were 10 births (6 boys and 4 girls) and 1 marriage by the grace of God. Below are testimonies from year 1 of Gifted.

----- TESTIMONY #1 (Kenya) -----

GIFTED. It's been such a blessing. It took me a long time to write this because I would often pause and cry. When I joined GIFTED, my expectations were that it would help me with my new-born daughter who is my second born child. I didn't for a moment fathom that it would have an effect on my relationship with my 8-year old son. All I knew was that I didn't want to fail as a mother in raising my daughter probably because I had failed with my son and lost hope in ever redeeming our relationship. My experience in GIFTED surpassed my expectations, redeeming the failed relationship I had with my son. For the first time in 8years (his whole life) the start of this year marked the first of many "I LOVE YOU's" to ever have been said from me to my son. GIFTED has moulded me in my walk with God and as a mother. My greatest testimony is how it went over its mandate to touch the life of my son. The teachings on parenthood will definitely be passed down to my children so that my grandkids can be raised right. Thank you GIFTED. You have been a blessing to me and a gift to my children.

----- TESTIMONY #2 (England) -----

GIFTED exceeded my expectations. This platform has been such a blessing and it has allowed us mums to delve into all sorts of topics with no boundaries or filters. Having a trusted space where we could let out our inner scars and fears without being judged but rather feeling the love has been awesome. The advice was 100% centred on Christ: everything was always and completely aligned with the Word of God. It was an open platform and no question was too silly to ask. We had a multitude of questions. I especially loved seeing all of the different milestones when a baby was born and suddenly they are 6 months old or 1 year old and you saw a mama who was so clueless at the start f her journey embracing the role and blossoming into being the best they could be. It has truly been wonderful and I won't ever forget this experience.

----- TESTIMONY #3 (England) -----

For me GIFTED was a place where I saw that I am not alone in this fight of motherhood. It's a place where I found that it's okay to be yourself and face the struggle with others. I am not a very talkative or outgoing person but I knew there were people praying for me and wishing me well. GIFTED gave me people to care about and pray for and just be in amazement watching families blossom and God really working. Thank you so much Minister Shammah for giving us this platform.

----- TESTIMONY #4 (England) -----

I joined GIFTED at a time when motherhood was still so fresh to me. My emotions were all over the place and felt like I had absolutely no idea what I was doing. GIFTED was created at the right time. I have "met" a lot of amazing women and I have gained so much more confidence in myself and in my mothering due to the love, support and encouragement that was expressed daily in the group. I am in awe to have been a part of something so wonderful but more importantly something that was so greatly needed. GIFTED has been a true blessing. I am always learning and growing, not only as a mother but as a woman of God and I am beyond grateful for such a sisterhood.

----- TESTIMONY #5 (Zimbabwe) -----

WOW GIFTED where to begin!? I remember scrolling through Instagram & coming across an Instagram post by Minister Shammah talking about her intention to start GIFTED. This post changed my life because at the time I was secretly pregnant only to the knowledge of my sister & then boyfriend. I excitedly and nervously joined a group of women who knew absolutely nothing about me (boy was I glad!) but who today, many months later know absolutely everything about me!

I particularly remember the time towards my traditional marriage when I had no idea what "attire" to purchase for the bedroom - the GIFTED women were my go to ladies pouring in advice accompanied with pictures to help guide me in my purchases and preparations for my wedding night. However things quickly went south & GIFTED gave me the courage to walk away from an ungodly & abusive relationship (before it got to marriage) even though I was pregnant & boldly choose God & His plans for me no matter the taboo that society & my culture places on single motherhood.

GIFTED was always a WhatsApp away no matter the time of day or night to help me navigate through the process of healing, letting go of bitterness & completely putting my trust in God for the future of me & my baby. I learnt to be intentional about praying for myself & child.

I was the last mother in GIFTED to give birth - me & my son were detained from leaving hospital. Due to an emergency c-section my final bill skyrocketed and I couldn't afford to pay it. One of the Mums in the group sent me several hundred dollars to assist in my bill & we were discharged! On top of that I received a further several hundred dollars 1 week after leaving the hospital which all of the mums raised to help me & my baby. I love that we could be open, vulnerable and freely let our emotions out in the group. Minister Shammah you've changed our lives forever - you have touched generations through this group and we will miss being on the same platform with you with your wisdom and great sense of humour as you move on to start a fresh year. God bless you for the seed you've sown in us.

----- **TESTIMONY #6 (England)** -----

GIFTED was an answer to a prayer that I never knew I needed until I became a part of it. Prior to becoming a mother, I heard many people say you need a tribe/ a village when raising kids. Well a tribe of Godly, amazing, beautiful intelligent women found me. The outpouring of love, the testimonies, the prayers, the laughter and the sisterhood I have found in this group shows me that God really loves me. He loves me so much that He sent a tribe of sisters to help me to be better, to challenge me to seek God daily, to pray fiercely for my family and to value myself as a wife and a mother. There were days when tears were my best friend and GIFTED got me through. We have never met in person but our sisterhood is strong and I'm truly grateful for the lifelong friendships I've found in this group. Thank you GIFTED for truly being a gift that keeps on giving!

----- **TESTIMONY #7 (Zimbabwe)** -----

My time in GIFTED was one of my most rewarding moments as a Christian. It helped me to have a better relationship with God. I now read more of the Bible, listen to more sermons & I am striving to be a better person in Christ everyday to those around me especially to my husband and my son. There was always priceless advice given by the ladies who always had kind words to say even in the worst of situations. In GIFTED ladies were completely open. I learned so many things that I have been able to pass on to other women and mothers alike. I have found lifetime friends and sisters though we have never met in person. God bless.

----- **TESTIMONY #8 (England)** -----

For me, GIFTED was a community and sisterhood. It was a period for me when my first child was only a few months old, so I was just learning how to navigate motherhood. Along with my other commitments such as a full-time job and studying - it was a lot to deal with which could have made or broken me. But having sisters to turn to, for wisdom, sound godly advice, to redirect you to God; the one true healer, mender, advisor and closest friend as well as a wealth of information about my baby worries! It was and still is just what I need. It's a place I felt I could be vulnerable, open, and also share my thoughts, and advice as we were all in different stages and coming from different walks of life, so we could all learn from one another. I have learned so much which has changed me for the better and impacted my walk with God. I've made sisters for life and I have no doubt that as it continues each group will benefit greatly and have testimonies to share!

----- TESTIMONY #9 (Italy) -----

I was informed of GIFTED by a friend. Initially I was not buying to the idea because I am not a fan of social media. But I got more interested when she told me it was piloted by Minister Shammah whom she had already told me a lot about.

But on joining I realized Minister Shammah was not enough reason but God himself had planned that I meet wonderful people with whom I could journey on in my new walk as a mother. I have had the opportunity to meet ladies filled with the knowledge of God.

GIFTED encouraged me to continue fixing my eyes on Jesus because only He makes life meaningful. One other thing that left a mark in my heart is how some women blended motherhood with their various ministries and callings. It encouraged me to pick myself up and not to relent at all in doing what God called me to do before making me a mother. I am grateful to God for allowing me to meet wonderful souls.

----- TESTIMONY #10 (Scotland) -----

GIFTED started shortly after I had my boy. Giving birth was my most rewarding yet demanding achievement to date. Being a first-time mum,

I had prepared myself both physically and mentally for labour but I soon got to realise that after birth is where the real work starts. It is a hands-on job with so much going on from body changes, breastfeeding woos, lack of sleep, fussy babies, teething, waiting for baby poo ...I could go on and on.

The point is, I needed to talk to mothers who had been there or who were going through the same changes in real time like I was. I am so grateful to God that He led me to GIFTED. I can proudly say that we might be millions of miles apart but just a text away. Every mother is so special and strong. There will always be help and advice given for anything.

GIFTED is more than a group of mothers giving baby advice, it's a sisterhood with a common understanding of Jesus Christ as our Lord & Saviour. He is the centre of our conversations, His Word our guide. There is no judgment only pure love. We have shared laughter, joy, happy moments, tears, cute baby photos, bad hair days, yummy recipes, prophecies, more babies-nothing is left out. We are an army of godly mums raising kings and queens of the kingdom.

----- ***TESTIMONY #11 (Scotland)*** -----

I joined GIFTED when I was about 3 weeks gone. I had been trying to have a baby and once it happened I needed all the right information I could get. GIFTED was more than an information platform, it was a community of women with so much in common and so much to learn from each-other in relationships, marriage, family & worship with God.

GIFTED helped me grow spiritually, it helped me during my weak times and struggles. One could share just about anything and you would be sure about its secrecy and you getting the right encouragement you needed to move on. I didn't say much on the platform because I didn't really have much to dish out in terms of experience but what I took out from GIFTED will last me a lifetime.

GIFTED helped me cope with treating lupus while pregnant, helped me in restoring my marriage, helped me with letting go and forgiving something I've been holding on to for years & also GIFTED helped me during my child delivery. God bless Minister Shammah for this platform and every mama on the group for being such a blessing to my family.

----- TESTIMONY #12 (England) -----

Having sisters in Christ who you can be open to is a rare thing and in the GIFTD group I've seen Gods love in so many ways. As a new mummy you have so many questions! You could literally post your question/thought at anytime of the day or night in the group and someone would respond to you. Whether the topic was personal, baby, marriage, health or just life in general. They would all stand with you in prayer and give you Word based advice. Honestly I've grown so much in a lot of things I was questioning myself about prior. I've been just so blessed to be a part of GIFTED.

----- TESTIMONY #13 (England) -----

Being part of GIFTED is the best thing that I never knew was missing in my journey as a mother. I have never in my life felt so welcomed into a group as much as I was into this one which just shows that God has a purpose when he gave Minister Shammah the vision about creating such a powerful platform for mothers to come together and help guide each other through the journey of pregnancy and motherhood. It has been a blessing to both me and my son and these wonderful GIFTED women have helped me raise him.

This group of women has been there whenever I needed advice. They have been there through the ups and the downs, always with the best words of encouragement and scriptures that really resonated with what I was going through. I have learned that God will send you what you need in your life at exactly the right time. What made this group even better is that it was filled with women who stand in Christ no matter what situation they are going through and I have seen some great things happen during this time.

I have been encouraged to continue my journey as a Christian and strengthen my faith in Christ. They have taught me that being a single mum is nothing to be ashamed of. I have developed friendships in this group that will last a lifetime. Truly GIFTED is a gift that keeps on giving. And thank you so much Minister Shammah for letting me be a part of it.

----- TESTIMONY #14 (Tanzania) -----

I still remember the email I sent to Minister Shammah requesting to join GIFTED and the 3 other Instagram DM's asking whether I had made it to the group due to her silence since my initial request. I'm sure at this point Minister Shammah was rolling her eyes like 'girl chill' but I just knew within me that I had to be a part of this group.

Now as much as testimonials might mean sugar coating certain experiences, I would like to attest that everything written by me and the other mothers is the absolute truth. I love the sense of sisterhood we had -always being available when one needed help.

I have a few other WhatsApp groups I am a part of but this is the one I made sure to read word of word every missed article, message (hundreds by the way), ebook and also to watch every sermon Minister Shammah would recommend we watch even if I had not been online for 3 days. I loved the jokes and the information shared. I say this with confidence, GIFTED has truly built me.

Minister Shammah, thank you for obeying God for us. Look at the beautiful sisterhood that was created.

ABOUT THE AUTHOUR

Minister Shammah Gara is a mother, preacher & teacher of the Word of God, worship leader, authour, girls' mentor as well as a businesswoman. Originally from Zimbabwe, she lives in the UK with her two children Tiiana & Isaac. She has a passion for all things prayer & for seeing God's daughters restored, walking in wholeness and the fullness of their destiny. She is also the founder of Girls On The Front Line Ministries which meets several times a week for 5am prayer via a conference call. Minister Shammah also runs a 12-week mentorship course for women aged 18-35 called 'Becoming A Girl of Purpose.'

CONNECT WITH MINISTER SHAMMAH

INFO.MINISTERSHAMMAH@GMAIL.COM

Shammah Gara **@shammahgara** **@handwritingofheaven**

BOOKING A 1-2-1 SESSION WITH MINISTER SHAMMAH

Every so often in life we all need a listening ear, an honest heart as well as an understanding mind to turn to when we are faced with decision making. Minister Shammah is here for you. Using the Word of God, her prophetic gifts & the almost 10 years of experience she has in helping women navigate through their walk with God, relationships, friendships, pain & all areas of life, Minister Shammah aims to support you in making sense of what the wise & godly step to take is in your current situation. No issue is too big or small. To book a session as well as have a read of the testimonials of women who have had sessions with her in the past please visit:

MINISTERSHAMMAH.SIMPLYBOOK.IT

FOR ANY OTHER BOOKINGS PLEASE EMAIL:
INFO.MINISTERSHAMMAH@GMAIL.COM

GIRLS ON THE FRONT LINE

Girls On The Front Line began in November 2015 after the Lord spoke to Shammah Gara *(The Founder)* and gave her an instruction one evening to gather girls who would commit to a lifestyle of prayer every single day. The words PURPOSE, PRAYER & POWER were highlighted in her Spirit & consequently a Skype conference group was formed consisting of girls from all over the world *(UK, Ireland, Italy, USA, South Africa, Zimbabwe, Germany, Turkey & Ghana)* who began meeting every single day 7days a week at a set time for a minimum of 30minutes to pray for themselves, their families & their nations based on varying weekly topics & themes. The Lord further confirmed this through several dreams in the days that followed the initial instruction.

Girls On The Front Line has a very clear mission statement:

1) To **LEAD** Girls back to the first port of call for all of life's situations: God. {***Zechariah 1:3***}
2) To **GUIDE** Girls in establishing, maintaining & strengthening their personal relationship with God. {***Luke 10:27***}
3) To RA**ISE** Girls who will be effective PRAYER warriors for themselves, their families & their nations. {***Psalm 144:1***}
4) To **HELP** Girls who carry PURPOSE walk into & fulfil their destinies with boldness in total freedom from darkness & the chains of the past. {***John 8:36***}
5) To **TEACH** Girls how to live lives of consistent victory & POWER over the enemy. {***Luke 10:19***}

Handwriting of Heaven

Printed in Poland
by Amazon Fulfillment
Poland Sp. z o.o., Wrocław